Financial Crises - Challenges and Solutions

Edited by Razali Haron

Published in London, United Kingdom

Financial Crises - Challenges and Solutions
http://dx.doi.org/10.5772/intechopen.100830
Edited by Razali Haron

Contributors
Heru Rahadyan, Alex Cukierman, Noor Zahirah Mohd Sidek, Jamilah Laidin, Qingxia (Jenny) Wang, Emna Trabelsi, Lethiwe Nzama, Thanda Sithole, Sezer Bozkus Kahyaoglu

First published in London, United Kingdom, 2023 by IntechOpen
IntechOpen is the global imprint of INTECHOPEN LIMITED, registered in England and Wales, registration number: 11086078, 5 Princes Gate Court, London, SW7 2QJ, United Kingdom
Printed in Croatia

British Library Cataloguing-in-Publication Data
A catalogue record for this book is available from the British Library

Additional hard and PDF copies can be obtained from orders@intechopen.com

Financial Crises - Challenges and Solutions
Edited by Razali Haron
p. cm.

This title is part of the Business, Management and Economics Book Series, Volume 12
Topic: Economics
Series Editor: Taufiq Choudhry
Topic Editor: Jaime Ortiz

Print ISBN 978-1-80356-866-9
Online ISBN 978-1-80356-867-6
eBook (PDF) ISBN 978-1-80356-868-3
ISSN 2753-894X

For EU product safety concerns:
IN TECH d.o.o., Prolaz Marije Krucifikse Kozulić 3, 51000 Rijeka, Croatia,
info@intechopen.com or visit our website at intechopen.com.

IntechOpen Book Series

Business, Management and Economics

Volume 12

Aims and Scope of the Series

This series will provide a comprehensive overview of recent research trends in business and management, economics, and marketing. Topics will include asset liability management, financial consequences of the financial crisis and covid-19, financial accounting, mergers and acquisitions, management accounting, SMEs, financial markets, corporate finance and governance, managerial technology and innovation, resource management and sustainable development, social entrepreneurship, corporate responsibility, ethics and accountability, microeconomics, labour economics, macroeconomics, public economics, financial economics, econometrics, direct marketing, creative marketing, internet marketing, market planning and forecasting, brand management, market segmentation and targeting and other topics under business and management. This book series will focus on various aspects of business and management whose in-depth understanding is critical for business and company management to function effectively during this uncertain time of financial crisis, Covid-19 pandemic, and military activity in Europe.

Meet the Series Editor

Prof. Choudhry holds a BSc degree in Economics from the University of Iowa, as well as a Masters and Ph.D. in Applied Economics from Clemson University, USA. In January 2006, he became a Professor of Finance at the University of Southampton Business School. He was previously a Professor of Finance at the University of Bradford Management School. He has over 80 articles published in international finance and economics journals. His research interests and specialties include financial econometrics, financial economics, international economics and finance, housing markets, financial markets, among others.

Meet the Volume Editor

Associate Professor Dr. Razali Haron holds a DBA and MBA and is currently the head of Responsible Research and Innovation at the International Islamic University Malaysia (IIUM) Institute of Islamic Banking and Finance. He has more than 15 years of extensive experience in the corporate sector covering equity fund management and capital market. His research interests are banking, corporate finance, and governance. He has numerous publications to his credit, including several edited books.

Contents

Preface **XIII**

Chapter 1 **1**
Inequality and the Environment: Impact and Way Forward
by Noor Zahirah Mohd Sidek and Jamilah Laidin

Chapter 2 **19**
Investors' Greed and Fear: An Event Study of Analyst Recommendations
by Qingxia (Jenny) Wang

Chapter 3 **37**
Currency and Banking Crises: The Origins and How to Identify Them
by Heru Rahadyan

Chapter 4 **57**
Current Challenges to World Financial Stability: To What Extent is the Past a Guide for the Future?
by Alex Cukierman

Chapter 5 **73**
Central Bank Transparency and Speculative Attacks: An Overview and Insights from a Laboratory Experiment in Tunisia
by Emna Trabelsi

Chapter 6 **93**
Asymmetric TVP-VAR Connectedness Approach: The Case of South Africa
by Lethiwe Nzama, Thanda Sithole and Sezer Bozkus Kahyaoglu

Preface

Financial crises continue to occur from time to time due to several factors affecting the world economy. These crises are becoming even more complex in parallel with rapid technological development, the complexity within financial assets, and contagion effects.

In seven chapters, Financial Crises – Challenges and Solutions examines the financial crises that are taking place globally and proposes possible solutions.

In Chapter 1, "Inequality and the Environment: Impact and Way Forward", Noor Zahirah Mohd Sidek and Jamilah Laidin examine the impact of income inequality on environmental pollution in 120 countries. The authors affirm the relationship between income inequality and environmental pollution for lower-middle- and low-income countries and propose policies to cushion the impact of income inequality to enable more allocation for environmental protection. This includes measures to reduce carbon dioxide (CO2) emissions.

In Chapter 2, "Investors' Greed and Fear: An Event Study of Analyst Recommendations", Qingxia (Jenny) Wang investigates the behaviour of stock returns from investors' reactions to analyst recommendations and finds the existence of abnormal stock returns around analyst recommendation. The author further documents that the magnitudes of abnormal returns are larger for NASDAQ compared to the NYSE.

In Chapter 3, "Currency and Banking Crises: The Origins and How to Identify Them", Heru Rahadyan provides evidence that crises can occur in any good or bad economic conditions, as they can be triggered by rational actions, panics, or contagion effects, and hence they should be mitigated with different policies. The author also proposes measures to identify the crises because once the crises are identified, determinants can be investigated.

In Chapter 4, "Current Challenges to World Financial Stability: To What Extent is the Past a Guide for the Future?", Alex Cukierman discusses current challenges to world financial stability considering lessons that have been learned from past financial crises. The author concludes that although there are similarities between the current and past crises, the current situation nonetheless differs in several important aspects. Further, recent developments in Fintech and the global economic disruptions caused by the war in Ukraine create novel financial vulnerabilities that differ from previous financial crises.

In Chapter 5, "Central Bank Transparency and Speculative Attacks: An Overview and Insights from a Laboratory Experiment in Tunisia", Emna Trabelsi discusses the use of experimental economics as an innovative tool to introduce economic issues in relation to speculative attacks. The author designed a laboratory experiment involving students to test theoretical predictions and proposed policy implications regarding optimal tools for information disclosure.

Finally, in Chapter 6, "Asymmetric TVP-VAR Connectedness Approach: The Case of South Africa", Lethiwe Nzama, Thanda Sithole, and Sezer Bozkus Kahyaoglu assess the connectedness of critical financial variables within the South African context and provide evidence of a connection between commodity prices and precious metals in international markets, as well as examine the exchange rates of the countries supplying the commodities and their risk indicators. The study is crucial for the economic policy of South Africa.

We owe this book's success to the chapter authors whose contributions are very much appreciated and acknowledged. We would also like to thank Karmen Đaleta of IntechOpen for her help throughout the publication process.

Razali Haron
IIUM Institute of Islamic Banking and Finance,
International Islamic University Malaysia,
Kuala Lumpur, Malaysia

Chapter 1

Inequality and the Environment: Impact and Way Forward

Noor Zahirah Mohd Sidek and Jamilah Laidin

Abstract

Economic and financial crisis thwarts the process of global economic growth, development, integration, and efforts to promote a sustainable environment. The onset of the recent crisis aggravates the problem of inequality and more resources need to be channeled for economic recovery. This study attempts to examine the impact of income inequality on environmental pollution in a sample of an unbalanced panel of 120 countries which consist of 42 high-income, 35 upper-middle-income, and 43 lower-middle- and low-income countries. The sample period runs from 1985 to 2019. The empirical results are quantitatively robust to a different alternative of proxy. Results affirmed an inverted *U*-shaped relationship between income inequality and environmental pollution for lower-middle- and low-income countries. The Environmental Kuznets Curve (EKC) hypothesis is present in the case of upper-middle, lower-middle- and low-income countries but not for high-income countries. The policy implication based on these findings is policies must be coordinated to cushion the impact of income inequality to enable more allocation for environmental protection such as measures to reduce carbon dioxide (CO2) emissions. Despite the crisis and economic slowdown, countries should take the opportunity to review their recovery plans by incorporating environmental concerns.

Keywords: CO_2 emission, methane, income inequality, environmental protection expenditure, economic recovery

1. Introduction

The persistent international community's attention and urgency towards reducing carbon impact on the environment have prompted various efforts from countries in the form of green policies, green financing, green investments, recycling, upcycling, and even the promotion of a circular economy. These efforts were briefly thwarted by the sudden COVID-19 outbreak. Following the COVID-19 pandemic, lockdowns in various parts of the world saw a significant reduction in carbon dioxide emissions from vehicles and factories. But this is only for a short-lived period. As vaccine rollout continues, economic activities begin to move towards full force albeit with major changes in the working mechanisms to comply with the new norms. In 2022, the Russian-Ukraine war disrupted the supply chain in the region, coupled with the rise in oil and commodity prices, the stock market bull-run, crypto winter, and inflation, recovery is further challenged [1–5]. As most countries pave their way towards recovery along with these challenges, the green agenda needs to align with the current situation such that policymakers could deploy bold measures to ensure sustainability in both the economy and the environment.

One of the major concerns is the possibility of inequality worsening as countries continue to recover. Some countries are rebounding faster than others although uncertainties are high due to the recurrence of pandemic waves and newfound COVID-19 variants. On one hand, the pandemic drove 120 million people to poverty as part of the consequences of the global recession. On a different note, the pandemic saw an increase in the wealth of billionaires and the emergence of post-COVID-19 billionaires and millionaires which illustrates the unequal effect of the pandemic on different groups of people. To partially cushion the impact of the recession and to reduce inequalities, governments have responded by introducing various policies, programs, grants, and subsidies for the marginalized groups and all sectors affected by the pandemic. Rescue packages along with vaccination rollouts are the main economic recovery agenda for all countries. Whether the green agenda will remain imperative or be temporarily put aside to focus more on economic recovery would depend on how inequalities affect expenditures on environmental protection. Thus, understanding the nature of how income inequality affects environmental pollution based on experience and historical data would assist future economic planning. As such, this study examines the impact of income inequality on environmental pollution in a sample of 120 countries.

The contribution of this study is twofold. First, the sample is disaggregated according to the level of income to better understand how income inequalities in countries with similar income thresholds affect environmental pollution. Second, to capture the possible indirect effects of inequality on environmental pollution, three multiplicative interactive interaction terms between income inequality vis-à-vis GDP, trade, and government environment expenditures. If income inequality is the product of economic growth or trade, then policies should be coordinated accordingly to account for such interactions. Therefore, understanding these issues is vital to ensure appropriate policy formulation to cope with post-pandemic development.

This study is organized in the following manner. The next section briefly reviews selected literature on environmental pollution and income inequalities. The third section narrates the theoretical consideration for this study, the estimation method, and discusses the nature of the data. The penultimate section provides the results and discussion, and the final section concludes.

2. Review of selected literature

In earlier literature, income inequality and environmental pollution are by-products of economic development and growth. The Kuznets Curve theory is often used to describe the relationship between income inequality and economic growth whilst the Environmental Kuznets Curve (EKC) is used to describe the relationship between environmental pollution which is normally captured by carbon dioxide (CO2) emission. The original Kuznets Curves hypothesized an inverted U-shaped association between economic growth and income inequality. The main assumption of this model is that at earlier stages of economic development income inequality is expected to increase as income levels increase. After reaching a certain threshold or inflection point, economic growth would lead to lower inequality as more redistribution takes place. This model implies that sustained economic growth and development would eventually reduce the problem of income inequality [6]. This model has been empirically tested extensively using different estimation methods, different sample periods, and a different sample of countries. Kuznets hypothesis was present in regional and country-specific studies, such as Thailand [7], Latin American countries [8], Africa [9], and counties in the US [10].

EKC proposed an inverted U-shaped relationship between economic growth denoted by income and environmental pollution as captured by CO2 emission. The EKC purports that as economic development makes its way, environmental pollution will increase due to higher production in the manufacturing, energy, and agriculture sector. After reaching a certain point, the relationship reverses as industries embrace renewable energy and more sustainable production mechanism. The efficacy of EKC is tested in various studies (*inter alia* [11–14]) and results infer the existence of EKC. Farhani and Ozturk [15], however, found a positive monotonic association between real GDP and CO2 emission which negates the existence of EKC. Shahbaz et al. [14] find mixed results where certain African countries like Tunisia, Zambia follows the EKC hypothesis whilst others such as Sudan and Tanzania experienced a *U*-shaped relationship between per capita CO2 and GDP.

Based on the previous literature, studies on the impact of income inequality on environmental pollution can be divided into three categories. The first group of studies found that income inequality lowers environmental quality, whilst the second group found evidence that income inequality improves environmental qualities. The third category argues that both positive and negative effects exists, such that the results are inconclusive. Differences may be due to the use of various data sets, econometric methods, or indices of income inequality, the results are mixed. Based on data from Turkey from 1984 to 2014, Uzar and Eyuboglu [16] demonstrate that income inequality has a positive impact on CO2 emissions and that the EKC is applicable in Turkey. The same conclusion is drawn by Baek and Gweisah [17] and Kasuga and Takaya [18]. In a sample of 217 countries, Wan et al. [19] found that the relationship between income inequality and CO_2 emissions is negative in high-income economies vis-à-vis the middle-high-income, middle-low-income, and low-income economies. Demir et al. [20] and Khan et al. [11] echoed the same conclusion. On the other hand, Uddin et al. [21], found that in the case of G7, the effect of income inequality on CO_2 emissions was significantly positive for the years 1870–1880 but significantly negative for the years 1950–2000. According to Belaïd et al. [22], who conducted a cross-sectional analysis of 11 Mediterranean nations, there is a long-term, significant and negative relationship between income inequality and per capita carbon emissions. This relationship suggests that greater inequality may prevent environmental degradation. Results, however, indicate that there is a short-term, positive, and significant correlation between income disparity and CO2 emissions.

Government expenditures are often viewed as a means to partly remedy the problems of inequality and environmental pollution. Government environment protection expenditure, for example, is a vital tool to ensure environmental quality (inter alia [23, 24]). The effect of government environment expenditures and environmental policies may be direct and indirect. Lopez et al. (2011) identified four main channels through which government expenditures may affect levels of pollution which are (i) the need for economic growth expands production which pressures the environment, (ii) human-intensive production harms the environment more vis-à-vis capital-intensive production, (iii) better use technology improves the technique of production, hence, causing less harm to the environment and (iv) higher income and better awareness of the environment raise the demand for better environmental quality and sustainable production. Empirical results are mixed with evidence of larger government expenditure lowering pollution (for example [25, 26]) and some showing higher pollution (for example [27, 28]). Grossman and Krueger [29] argue that differences in results may be due to countries being at different points of the EKC. However, it should be noted that the majority of earlier studies use total government expenditure as a proxy which is for other uses and not specifically for environmental protection. More data on environmental protection expenditure would enable more specific analysis. Existing studies do not account for the interactive effect of government expenditures and income inequality which could be a possible explanation of the indirect effect of government environment expenditure and pollution. This gap is addressed in this study.

3. Methodology

This section explores some theoretical considerations based on the EKC model to identify the baseline empirical model. The next sub-section identifies the estimation method followed by a discussion on the data sources, control variables, and variables for robustness tests.

3.1 Theoretical considerations

The Environmental Kuznets Curve (EKC) describes the possibility of an inverted *U*-shaped relationship between environmental pollution and economic growth. As the economy progress via an increase in income, pollution is hypothesized to increase until it reaches a certain inflection point where pollution began to decrease [29]. In the early stages of economic development, it is assumed that industrialization would take place and contribute a large percentage towards GDP growth. Industrialization is expected to use large amounts of energy which results in environmental pollution in the form of CO2 emissions. CO2 emission stems from (i) burning of fossil fuels such as burning solid, liquid, gas fuel, or gas flaring, or from the production of cement, (ii) production of electricity and heat production, (iii) liquid fuel consumption for example the use of petroleum-derived fuels, (iv) combustion of fuels from the manufacturing (for example from coke inputs to blast furnaces) and construction sectors, (v) solid fuel consumption from the use of coal, (vi) transport activities such as aviation, domestic navigation, road, rail and pipeline transport, and (vi) use of natural gas. In the agriculture sector, greenhouse gas emissions from livestock, such as cows, rice, wheat, and corn production contribute to pollution. Other forms of pollution include methane which is emitted during the production and transport of coal or natural gas, from livestock such as cows, and the decay of waste in the soil.

As the economy progressed and began wealth accumulation, countries would be able to invest in research and development (R&D) towards the production of machines and mechanisms that could minimize the impact on the environment. Examples include the use of green technology in production. As a result, even as the economy continues to progress, the impact on the environment is minimized. Another reason for the possible decline in pollution is due to both public and private awareness of the negative impact of pollution left unchecked. International organizations such as the United Nations, World Bank, and the International Monetary Funds have made concerted efforts on environmental sustainability such as the use of renewable energy and the promotion of a circular economy. Governments have come together towards embracing green policies and the adoption of greener technologies to reduce CO2 emissions. At a micro level, non-governmental organizations (NGOs) are also propagating reduction in environmental pollution via recycling, upcycling, and more recently, replacing the end-of-life concept with the restoration which leads to changes in business models, operations, systems, use of materials, and reduction in the use of harmful chemicals. In other words, producers are responsible for the whole lifecycle of the products.

In countries where inequality and poverty are prevalent, the poorer segment of the economy are more concerned with their survival, therefore, have less interest in environmental policies or programs [30] unless they can monetize from the policies. For example, via the collection of paper, glass, or tin that could be sold to recycling industries. According to the Median Voter Theory, poorer societies are more concerned with material wellbeing and would be less interested to support environmental related policies [31]. Ridzuan [32] (2019) suggests that society's interest in environmental protection could be downplayed if income inequalities are predominant within the society. On a similar note, Franzen and Meyer [33] and Facchini et al. [34] argued that when income inequality is high, the public is more concerned focused on economic growth and redistribution compared to environmental issues. Consequently, income inequality reduces government expenditures on environmental protection [35]. On the other hand, the richer segment of the society could easily fulfill their daily needs and have excess wealth which could be directed towards the consumption of environmentally friendly products and comply with other environmentally friendly policies.

3.2 Estimation method

The System GMM (S-GMM) is used in this study to examine the impact of inequality and other control variables on environmental pollution. S-GMM overcomes the shortcomings of the standard GMM where biases increase the number of instruments proliferate and weak instrument problems, and the problem of poor finite sample properties in terms of bias and precision in Difference GMM and the problem of lagged levels [36]. S-GMM corrects endogeneity such as in *CO2* and *GDP* by introducing more instruments to considerably improve efficiency and transforms the instruments to make them uncorrelated (exogeneous) with the fixed effects, permits a certain degree of endogeneity in the other regressors and optimally combines information on cross country variation in levels with that on within-country variation in changes [37].

The baseline empirical model can be described as follows:

$$\begin{aligned} CO2_{it} = {} & \alpha_1 CO2_{it-1} + \beta_2 \log GDP_{it-1} + \beta_3 GDP^2_{it-1} + \beta_4 GDP_{gr_{it-1}} \\ & + \beta_5 Dom_{Credit_{it-1}} + \beta_6 Trade_{it-1} + \beta_7 Gini_{disp_{it-1}} + \rho_{it} + \varepsilon_{it} + v_{it} \end{aligned} \tag{1}$$

where $CO2_{it}$ denotes environmental pollution proxied by CO2 and methane emission for individual i in period t, $CO2_{i,t-1}$is the lagged of environmental pollution in the previous period and $\rho_{it} + \varepsilon_{it} + v_{it}$ represents the error components decomposition of the error term which allows for unobserved heterogeneity (ε_{it} hereafter). Other assumption includes $v_{i,t}$ is serially uncorrelated. The control variables include growth of GDP (*gdp_gr*), trade openness (*trade*), domestic credit (*dom_credit*), and a measure of inequality (*Gini_disp*). To empirically examine whether the effect of income inequality on CO2 emission is conditional on GDP, trade, and government environment expenditure, the baseline model is modified to incorporate a multiplicative interaction term of income inequality and the three variables which are the (i) size of the economy and income inequality ($GDP \times Gini\_disp$), (ii) the impact of trade on income inequality ($Trade \times Gini\_disp$) and (iii) the interaction of government expenditure on environment protection and income inequality ($GE \times Gini\_disp$) and (iv) the combined effect of economic growth and financial development on income inequality ($GDP \times Dom\_credit \times Gini\_disp$). The interaction models are as follows:

$$\begin{aligned} CO2_{it} = {} & \alpha_1 CO2_{it-1} + \beta_2 \log GDP_{it-1} + \beta_3 GDP^2_{it-1} + \beta_4 GDP_{gr_{it-1}} \\ & + \beta_5 Dom_{Credit_{it-1}} + \beta_6 Openness_{it-1} + \beta_7 Gini_{disp_{it-1}} \\ & + \beta_8 \left(GDP \times Gini_{disp}\right)_{it-1} + \rho_{it} + \varepsilon_{it} + v_{it} \end{aligned} \tag{2}$$

$$\begin{aligned} CO2_{it} = {} & \alpha_1 CO2_{it-1} + \beta_2 \log GDP_{it-1} + \beta_3 GDP^2_{it-1} + \beta_4 GDP_{gr_{it-1}} \\ & + \beta_5 Dom_{Credit_{it-1}} + \beta_6 Openness_{it-1} + \beta_7 Gini_{disp_{it-1}} \\ & + \beta_8 \left(Trade \times Gini_{disp}\right)_{it-1} + \rho_{it} + \varepsilon_{it} + v_{it} \end{aligned} \tag{3}$$

$$\begin{aligned} CO2_{it} = {} & \alpha_1 CO2_{it-1} + \beta_2 \log GDP_{it-1} + \beta_3 GDP^2_{it-1} + \beta_4 GDP_{gr_{it-1}} \\ & + \beta_5 Dom_{Credit_{it-1}} + \beta_6 Openness_{it-1} + \beta_7 Gini_{disp_{it-1}} + \beta_8 (GE \\ & \times Gini_{disp})_{it-1} + \rho_{it} + \varepsilon_{it} + v_{it} \end{aligned} \tag{4}$$

3.3 Data

A panel of unbalanced data from 120 countries was chosen based on the availability of the focal variables which are CO2 and income inequality data. The sample ranges from 1985 to 2019, drawn from various datasets. The sample was further disaggregated according to the level of income to control for the effect of income and to ensure that inferences were made based on samples that belong to some similar criteria which is in this case, the level of income. The segregated sample consists of 42 high-income, 35 upper-middle-income, and 43 lower-middle- and low-income countries. Segregation of the sample allows analysis and comparison of the impact of the different variables on CO2. In addition, more specific results can be obtained based on the characteristics, conditions, and resources of countries with similar income levels. This would allow understanding the nature and degree of association amongst the variables. The sample was segregated into three categories of income which are high-income countries, upper-middle-income countries, and lower-middle- and low-income countries. The categorization is based on The World Economic Situation and Prospects (WESP), United Nations [38]. The list of countries is listed in Appendix I. Data on CO2 and methane were derived from the WDI, World Bank and Emissions Database for Global Atmospheric Research (EDGAR), European Commission.

Income inequality (*gini_disp*) is represented by the Gini coefficients derived from the Standardized World Income Inequality Database (SWIID) V9.1 originally by Solt [39, 40]. SWIID is the best available proxy for income inequality since it covers the longest period and the largest number of countries compared to other databases.

SWIID 9.1 provides Gini coefficients for market incomes and net incomes (disposable Gini) which allows for international comparison. For the purpose of this study, only disposable Gini is used since it is an after-tax Gini which is calculated after taking out the effect of taxes and after considering the effect of transfer payments. It should be noted that Gini coefficients are not available for all countries for the stipulated time, hence, regression is based on unbalanced panel data. Alternative measures of income inequality such as wage inequality or ratio inequality, market income (income before taxes and transfers), disposable income (household income after pensions, unemployment insurance, social assistance transfers, and other government cash benefits), post-tax income (gross income minus all direct and indirect taxes) and gross income (market income plus government cash benefits) are available albeit calculated differently. Nevertheless, the range of countries offered by these alternative proxies is limited to a few countries only, making extensive international comparison difficult. Therefore, SWIID is the best available proxy.

The proxy for income is real GDP from the World Development Indicator (WDI) database, World Bank which serves the role to control for the size of the economy and the EKC effects. GDP growth controls for the effect of the level of development where wealthier economies are presumed to have a larger public sector which is bound to affect the design of fiscal policy and redistribution. Wagner's Law stipulates that higher economic development would result in greater redistribution, which subsequently suppresses the problem of income inequality. According to Wagner, as economies developed, more resources are available for redistribution which later, promotes economic growth through higher income and increase aggregate demand [41]. Other control variables include domestic credit to capture financial development and trade openness to represent globalization and the effects of international market integration. Trade openness is defined as total imports plus export as a percentage of GDP. Both data were drawn from the WDI database. The role of government expenditure on the environment is captured by the amount of government expenditure on environment protection as a percentage of total government expenditure. Data is extracted from the Expenditure by Functions of Government (COFOG), Government Finance Statistics, and the International Monetary Fund (IMF).

4. Results and discussion

The descriptive and correlation statistics for all variables for 120 countries over the period of 1985 to 2019 are reported in **Tables 1** and **2**. Real GDP (*gdp*) and government environment protection expenditure (*gov_env*) are expressed in the logarithm. The correlation statistics in **Table 2** shows no high correlation amongst the variables.

Table 3 displays the overall results for the whole sample and high-income countries. The lagged values of CO2 emission are consistently significant across all models in the overall sample and the high-income countries. The proxy for economic growth, *gdp* is significant except for eq. 4 but gdp^2 is negative but insignificant. The results suggest that economic growth continues to increase CO2 emission in the overall sample and high-income countries. The presence of an inverted *U*-shaped EKC could not be established based on these results. The rate of economic growth is positive and significant for all regression but the same could be generalized in the case of high-income countries. The positive and significant impact of financial development as proxied by domestic credit (*dom_credit*) indicates how improvement in credit access, for example, promotes more production and hence, higher CO2 emission. Results are

Variable	Obs	Mean	Std. Dev.	Min	Max
CO_2	3722	4.9745	6.8144	0.0209	70.0422
methane	2893	23.4996	18.6431	−1.9	100.7621
gdp	4062	26.8479	28.0095	0.00	30.5379
gdp_gr	4044	43.4591	442.2550	−50.2481	6310.1350
dom_credit	3934	78.7938	54.0776	9.1358	442.6200
trade	3027	53.4148	47.7398	0	308.9784
gini_disp	3749	37.9002	8.8526	17.5	67.1000
gov_env	599	6.0662	7.2042	0	9.6216

Notes: gdp and gov_env are expressed in a logarithmic term.

Table 1.
Descriptive statistics.

	CO_2	Methane	gdp	gdp_gr	dom_credit	Trade	gini_disp	gov_env
CO_2	1							
methane	0.5722	1						
gdp	0.1001	0.1807	1					
gdp_gr	0.5339	0.3702	0.142	1				
dom_credit	0.1452	−0.1203	0.3716	−0.0664	1			
trade	0.0385	0.1689	−0.1557	0.1199	0.0637	1		
gini_disp	−0.1096	0.1022	−0.1187	0.0309	−0.1864	−0.0387	1	
gov_env	0.0158	−0.032	−0.1306	−0.0474	−0.0193	0.0768	−0.0807	1

Table 2.
Correlation.

consistent for the overall sample and high-income countries; results are significant for eqs. 1–3. International trade (*trade*) is not significant except for eq. 3 in the overall sample.

Table 4 illustrates the results for upper-middle and lower-middle- and low-income countries. In the case of upper-middle-income countries, lagged term of CO2 emission is positively related to CO2 emission which is in line with the use of S-GMM. Evidence of an inverted *U*-shaped EKC is present implying the existence of a certain threshold point where reduction of CO2 emission takes place with better use of technology and more sustainable production techniques. These results are consistent with Le and Nguyen [13], Shahbaz et al. [14], and Le et al. [12]. More financial development implies higher emission of CO2. For lower-middle- and low-income countries, *gdp* is positive and significant and *gdp2* is negative and significant which suggests the existence of an inverted U-shaped relationship between economic growth and CO2 emission. Domestic credit and trade openness have the expected sign which both positive and significant, indicating the growth of trade and financial development leads to increased CO2 emission, hence, environmental pollution. Results are fairly consistent across all specifications.

DOI: http://dx.doi.org/10.5772/intechopen.107246

Dependent variable: CO2 Emission								
Variable	**Overall sample**				**High-income countries**			
Panel	**1**	**2**	**3**	**4**	**1**	**2**	**3**	**4**
$CO2_{t-1}$	0.0942*** (0.0042)	0.9515*** (0.0053)	0.7211*** (0.0060)	0.9415*** (0.0095)	0.9412*** (0.0080)	0.9513*** (0.0095)	0.7312*** (0.0098)	0.9744*** (0.0287)
gdp	0.0670*** (0.0000)	−0.0552* (0.0000)	0.0441*** (0.0000)	0.0009 (0.0018)	0.0529** (0.0000)	0.0500* (0.0000)	0.0337*** (0.0000)	−0.0004 (0.0012)
gdp^2	−0.0098 (0.0120)	−0.0091 (.0121)	−0.0080 (0.0200)	−0.0060 (0.0120)	−0.0082 (0.0170)	−0.0065 (0.0150)	−0.0055** (0.0100)	−0.0025 (0.0101)
gdp_gr	0.0092** (0.0038)	0.0139* (0.0043)	0.0056** (0.0027)	0.0214 (0.0138)	0.0070 (0.0107)	0.0255* (0.0141)	0.0006 (0.0076)	0.0085 (0.0474)
dom_credit	0.0064*** (0.0010)	0.0065*** (0.0010)	0.0058*** (0.0007)	0.0077*** (0.0024)	0.0062*** (0.0016)	0.0058*** (0.0016)	0.0069*** (0.0011)	−0.0041 (0.0055)
trade	0.0010 (0.0008)	−0.0009 (0.0008)	0.0270*** (0.0008)	0.0029 (0.0019)	0.0011 (0.0013)	0.0013 (0.0013)	0.0269*** (0.0013)	0.0022 (0.0049)
gini_disp	0.0015* (0.0079)	0.0145** (0.0080)	0.0082 (0.0057)	1.3052*** (0.0329)	0.0130 (0.0218)	0.0080 (0.0221)	0.0366** (0.0157)	0.9024 (0.1316)
constant	1.0568*** (0.3338)	1.0011*** (0.3403)	2.6500*** (0.2454)	6.0514*** (1.3698)	1.1744* (0.6068)	0.9330 (0.6242)	1.8222*** (0.4356)	−1.9225 (5.8957)
gdp × gini_disp	—	0.0051*** (0.0001)		—	—	0.0326*** (0.0038)	—	—
trade × gini_disp	—		0.0052*** (0.0013)	—	—	—	0.0036** (0.0018)	—
gov_env × gini_disp	—	—	—	−0.5431*** (0.0153)	—	—	—	−0.695*** (0.0363)
Obs.	2376	2376	2376		862	862	862	98
Inst.	502	503	503		502	503	503	99

*Notes: Panels 1–4 are based on Eqs. 1–4. Standard errors are in parentheses. ***, ** and * denote 1%, 5%, and 10% significant levels.*

Table 3.
Impact of inequality on CO2 emission – Overall sample and high-income countries.

Dependent variable: CO2 emission								
Variable	**Upper middle-income countries**				**Lower middle- and low-income countries**			
	1	2	3	4	1	2	3	4
$CO2_{t-1}$	0.9421*** (0.0161)	0.9533*** (0.0158)	0.9421*** (0.0161)	0.9671*** (0.1816)	0.8839*** (0.0116)	0.6183*** (0.0108)	0.1499*** (0.0076)	0.5932*** (0.0216)
gdp	0.0244*** (0.0000)	0.0211*** (0.0000)	0.0115*** (8.000)	0.0079* (0.0000)	0.0021 (0.0000)	−.0042** (0.0018)	0.0001*** (0.0000)	0.0001*** (0.0000)
gdp^2	−0.0088*** (0.0000)	−0.0074*** (0.0000)	−0.0067*** (0.0000)	−0.0011** (0.0000)	−0.0021 (0.0000)	−0.0061** (0.0000)	−0.0055*** (0.0000)	−0.0005*** (0.0000)
gdp_gr	−0.0043 (0.0068)	−0.0031 (0.0068)	−0.0043 (0.0068)	−0.0254*** (0.0077)	0.0134*** (0.0023)	−0.0150*** (0.0019)	−0.0030*** (0.0008)	0.0551*** (0.0086)
dom_credit	0.0019** (0.0010)	0.0016* (0.0010)	0.0019** (0.0010)	−0.0002 (0.0022)	0.0047*** (0.0013	0.0068*** (0.0009)	0.0078* (0.0004)	0.0231*** (0.0031)
trade	0.00074 (0.0009)	0.0007 (0.0009)	0.0007 (0.0009)	0.0008 (0.0025)	0.0025*** (0.0008)	0.0005 (0.0006)	0.0090*** (0.0000)	−0.0006 (0.0028)
gini_disp	0.0022 (0.0048)	0.0022 (0.0048)	0.0022 (0.0048)	0.0043 (0.0087)	0.0270*** (0.0075)	0.0454*** (0.0057)	0.0182*** (0.0022)	0.1473*** (0.0177)
constant	0.0548 (0.2477)	0.0579 (0.2493)	0.0548 (0.2477)	−0.2871 (0.4236)	0.8999*** (0.3317)	—	1.3652*** (0.1179)	6.4432*** (0.8850)
gdp × gini_disp	—	0.0031*** (0.0001)		—	—	0.0218*** (0.0029)	—	—
trade × gini_disp	—		0.0027*** (0.0011)	—	—	—	0.0032** (0.0016)	—
gov_env × gini_disp	—	—	—	−0.3512*** (0.0153)	—	—	—	−0.0559*** (0.0243)
Obs.	691	691	691	177	823	823	823	118
Inst.	499	498	499	167	488	489	489	126

*Notes: Panels 1–4 are based on Eqs. 1–4. Standard errors are in parentheses. ***, ** and * denote 1%, 5%, and 10% significant levels.*

Table 4.
Impact of inequality on CO2 emission – Upper Middle, Lower Middle- and Low-Income Countries.

Dependent variable: CO2 emission								
Variable	**Overall sample**				**High income countries**			
Panel	**1**	**2**	**3**	**4**	**1**	**2**	**3**	**4**
$methane_{t-1}$	0.9118*** (0.0175)	0.9118*** (0.0175)	0.8548*** (0.0512)	0.9086*** (0.0176)	0.9605*** (0.0158)	0.8573*** (0.0138)	0.6221*** (0.1020)	0.9553*** (0.0158)
gdp	0.0075* (0.0100)	0.0063*** (0.0010)	0.0044*** (0.0011)	0.0025* (0.0011)	0.0069*** (0.0000)	0.0060*** (0.000)	0.0039 (0.0000)	0.0022*** (0.0000)
gdp^2	−0.0063** (0.0031)	−0.0045 (0.0100)	−0.0032 (0.0049)	−0.0011 (0.0079)	−0.0061** (0.0030)	−0.0042** (0.0030)	0.0034 (0.0060)	0.0010 (0.0030)
gdp_gr	0.0881*** (0.0174)	0.0961*** (0.0188)	0.0376 (0.0791)	0.0890*** (0.0174)	0.0291 (0.0269)	0.0483 (0.0367)	0.0049 (0.0783)	−0.0307 (0.0269)
dom_credit	0.0158** (0.0063)	0.0159** (0.0063)	0.0114 (0.0163)	0.0061** (0.0063)	0.0047 (0.0043)	0.0042 (0.0044)	−0.0006 (0.0150)	0.0053 (0.0043)
trade	0.0008 (0.0057)	0.0013 (0.0019)	0.0063 (0.0318)	−0.0028 (0.0063)	0.0036 (0.0032)	0.0037 (0.0032)	0.0120 (0.0303)	−0.0019 (0.0037)
gini_disp	0.1513*** (0.0432)	0.1516 (0.0432)	0.7270*** (0.1436	0.1624*** (0.0440)	0.0145 (0.0567)	0.0135 (0.0567)	0.8107 (0.8877)	0.0139 (0.0565)
constant	−4.1768** (1.7505)	−4.2485** (1.7507)	−4.0502*** (7.8713)	−4.5688 (1.7723)	1.1979 (1.7054)	1.2955 (1.7107)	−2.1245 (3.6437)	1.1483 (1.7013)
gdp × gini_disp	—	0.0063*** (0.0011)		—	—	0.0055*** (0.0027)	—	—
trade × gini_disp	—		0.0047*** (0.0022)	—	—	—	0.0041** (0.0023)	—
gov_env × gini_disp	—	—	—	−0.6429*** (0.2556)	—	—	—	−0.4761*** (0.0876)
Obs.	1557	1557	123	1557	544	544	36	544
Inst.	282	283	75	283	282	283	31	283

*Notes: Panels 1–4 are based on Eqs. 1–4. Standard errors are in parentheses. ***, ** and * denote 1%, 5%, and 10% significant levels.*

Table 5.
Impact of inequality on CO2 emission – Overall Sample and High-Income Countries.

Dependent variable: CO2 emission								
Variable	**Upper middle-income countries**				**Lower middle- and low-income countries**			
Panel	1	2	3	4	1	2	3	4
$methane_{t-1}$	0.8421*** (0.0239)	0.8420*** (0.0239)	0.8547*** (0.1325)	0.8420*** (0.0239)	0.8288*** (0.0256)	0.8292*** (0.0256)	0.7350*** (0.0786)	0.8332*** (0.0257
gdp	0.0055*** (0.0010)	0.0041*** (0.0010)	0.0030*** (0.0011)	0.0029** (0.0014)	0.0033*** (0.0015)	0.0030*** (0.0015)	0.0021*** (0.0000)	0.0010*** (0.0000)
gdp^2	−0.0041*** (0.0003)	−0.0038*** (0.0000)	−0.0035*** (0.0002)	−0.0010*** (0.0001)	−0.0035** (0.0030)	−0.0027** (0.0030)	0.0026*** (0.0001)	0.0009*** (0.0000)
gdp_gr	0.0047 (0.0082)	0.0032 (0.0642)	0.1045 (0.1309)	0.0032 (0.0642)	0.0803*** (0.0239)	0.0865*** (0.0267)	0.0388 (0.2934)	0.0710*** (0.0243)
dom_credit	0.0032* (0.0642)	0.0228** (0.0097)	0.0255 (0.0513)	0.0228** (0.0097)	0.0666*** (0.0200)	0.0686*** (0.0205)	0.0309 (0.1228)	0.0458*** (0.0224)
trade	0.0210** (0.0087)	0.0210** (0.0087)	0.0285 (0.0513)	0.0210* (0.0139)	0.0384*** (0.0116)	0.0396*** (0.1181)	0.0448 (0.1003)	0.0239* (3.7864)
gini_disp	0.1423** (0.0648)	1.4232** (0.0648)	0.00766 (0.2556)	1.4232** (0.0648)	0.4845*** (0.0870)	0.4829*** (0.0871)	1.8993*** (0.3646)	0.5215*** (0.0889)
constant	7.8854** (3.0638)	7.8854** (3.0638)	4.3003 (14.0168)	7.8854** (3.0638)	1.2699*** (3.75551)	1.2939*** (3.7581)	0.2749*** (17.2062)	2.2438 (3.7864)
gdp × gini_disp	—	0.0021*** (0.0001)		—	—	0.0019*** (0.0001)	—	—
trade × gini_disp	—		0.0024*** (0.0010)	—	—	—	0.0018** (0.0009)	—
gov_env × gini_disp	—	—	—	−0.0787*** (0.0332)	—	—	—	−0.0481*** (0.0111)
		—						
Obs.	446	446	48	446	567	567	39	567
Inst.	283	283	38	283	282	283	31	283

*Notes: Panels21qq 1–4 are based on Eqs. 1–4. Standard errors are in parentheses. ***, ** and * denote 1%, 5%, and 10% significant levels.*

Table 6.
Impact of inequality on CO2 emission – Upper Middle, Lower Middle- and Low-Income Countries.

The conditional effect of economic growth on income inequality ($gdp \times gini\_disp$) is positive and significant, inferring that CO2 emission could be aggravated if income inequality is high coupled with economic growth in all samples. The interaction between trade and income inequality is also positive and significant for all samples inferring the combined effects of international market integration and income inequality leads to more pollution. The third interaction variable between government environment expenditures and income inequality is negative and significant, suggesting the possibility of lower government environment expenditure given income inequality could increase CO2 emission. Results seem to support the Median Voter Theory that purported lower income inequality would lead to more interest in environmental pollution-related policies and public spending, hence, leading to lower pollution. These results are parallel to Magnani [35] and Kempf and Rossignol [31] albeit different sample, estimation technique, and data span. These results are also in line with Uzar [42] who suggests that a decline in income inequality will enhance the usage of renewable energy, leading to lower environmental pollutions due to CO2, SO2, methane, and other harmful emissions (**Table 5**).

Table 6 shows the modified estimations using methane to proxy for environmental pollution as a measure of robustness. Results are relatively consistent with the baseline results. Using methane as a proxy, high-income countries show some support of the inverted U-shaped EKC. Trade has positive and significant effect on methane emission in for upper-middle income countries and lower-middle and low-income countries. In tandem with the results in the baseline regression, financial development is consistently positive and significant, inferring increase financial development promotes more production and consumption, hence, increasing emission of methane.

5. Conclusion

This study re-examines the EKC by controlling for the level of development and growth, financial development, international market integration, and government expenditure on environment protection. Overall, the results lend support to the inverted U-shaped EKC in the case of upper-middle countries, lower-middle- and low-income countries. The same could not be concluded for high-income countries. In the case of high-income countries, the combination of public policies in the form of environmental regulations, indirect government subsidies, and continuous technological innovation to reduce pollution allows the non-contradictory co-existence between economic growth and checked environmental pollution. Moreover, the inverted U-shaped EKC appears to be non-applicable to high-income countries as these countries would have experienced the U-shaped phenomenon earlier than the period covered in this study. Higher-income inequality resulting in higher environmental pollution is statistically evident for the overall sample, high-income, and lower-middle- and low-income countries. Financial development is a vital indicator for CO2 emission, lending support for higher emissions as the financial sector develops and matures. International market integration as represented by trade openness is significant across all equations for lower-middle and low-income countries but only partially significant for other samples.

In conclusion, economic growth and development are partly fueled by financial development and trade leading to higher production and consumption which translates into environmental pollution. To curb pollution, government environmental expenditure should be the catalyst along with other green policies such as the use of renewable energy, responsible production, and consumption, implementation of the circular economy-type of policies, and enforcement. Reducing income inequality indicates better income and wealth redistribution. Thus, more government expenditure could be allocated and spent on maintaining and sustaining the environment rather than used to provide subsidies or transfers to the poorer section of the economy. Failure to address income inequality could impede efforts to reduce CO2 emissions and other efforts to reduce environmental degradation as the post-COVID-19 fiscal policies mostly focused on economic recovery with various efforts aimed to remedy the high unemployment, production, and supply chain disruptions due to the pandemic. Nevertheless, this can be viewed as an opportunity to restart production and the whole supply chain ecosystem in a more environmentally sustainable manner.

Appendix I. List of countries

High-Income countries

Australia, Austria, Barbados, Belgium, Canada, Croatia, Cyprus, Czech, Denmark, Estonia, Finland, France, Germany, Greece, Iceland, Ireland, Italy, Japan, Latvia, Lithuania, Luxembourg, Netherland, New Zealand, Poland, Portugal, Qatar, South Korea, Singapore, Hong Kong, Hungary, Israel, Norway, Panama, Slovak Republic, Slovenia, Spain, Sweden, Switzerland, United Kingdom, United States, Uruguay.

Upper middle-income countries

Albania, Algeria, Argentina, Armenia, Belarus, Botswana, Brazil, Bulgaria, China, Colombia, Costa Rica, Dominican Republic, Ecuador, Fiji, Georgia, Guatemala, Iran, Jamaica, Jordan, Kazakhstan, Malaysia, Mauritius, Mexico, Namibia, North Macedonia, Paraguay, Peru, Romania, Russian Federation, Serbia, South Africa, Sri Lanka, Thailand, Turkey, Venezuela.

Lower middle- and low-income countries

Bangladesh, Bolivia, Djibouti, Egypt, El Salvador, Ghana, Honduras, India, Indonesia, Kenya, Kyrgyzstan, Lao, Lesotho, Mauritania, Mongolia, Morocco, Nicaragua, Nigeria, Pakistan, Philippines, Senegal, Sudan, Tunisia, Ukraine, Vietnam, Zambia, Zimbabwe.

Burkina Faso, Burundi, Ethiopia, Gambia, Guinea, Madagascar, Malawi, Mozambique, Nepal, Niger, Rwanda, Sierra Leone, Tajikistan, Uganda, Tanzania, Yemen.

Author details

Noor Zahirah Mohd Sidek[1]* and Jamilah Laidin[2]

1 Faculty of Business and Management, Universiti Teknologi MARA, Sungai Petani, Kedah, Malaysia

2 Universiti Teknologi MARA, Sungai Petani, Kedah, Malaysia

*Address all correspondence to: kedah.uitm.edu.my

References

[1] Baffes J, Nagle P. Commodity prices surge due to the war in Ukraine. Let's Talk Development, World Bank. 2022. https://blogs.worldbank.org/developmenttalk/commodity-prices-surge-due-war-ukraine

[2] International Monetary Fund (IMF). Gloomy and more uncertain. World Economic Outlook. 2022. https://www.imf.org/en/Publications/WEO/Issues/2022/07/26/world-economic-outlook-update-july-2022

[3] Kharif O. Why another 'crypto winter' is test for digital money. Bloomberg. 2022. https://www.bloomberg.com/news/articles/2022-07-27/why-another-crypto-winter-is-test-for-digital-money-quicktake

[4] Powell F. Crypto winter is coming: What you need to know. Forbes Advisor. 2022. https://www.forbes.com/advisor/investing/cryptocurrency/what-is-crypto-winter/

[5] Read S. The 'crypto winter' is here. But what is it and what does it mean for the wider economy?. Financial and Monetary Systems, World Economic Forum. 2022. https://www.weforum.org/agenda/2022/06/cryptocurrency-crash-crypto-winter/

[6] Lyubimov I. Income inequality revisited 60 years later: Piketty vs Kuznets. Russian Journal of Economics. 2017;**3**(1):42-53

[7] Paweenawat SW, McNown R. The determinants of income inequality in Thailand: A synthetic cohort analysis. Journal of Asian Economics. 2014;**31**:10-21

[8] Thomas C. Income Inequality and economic development in Latin America: A test for the Kuznets inverted-u curve. Indian Journal of Economics and Business. 2015;**14**(1):143-161

[9] Meniago C, Asongu SA. Revisiting the finance-inequality nexus in a panel of African countries. Research in International Business and Finance. 2018;**46**:399-419

[10] Nielsen F, Alderson AS. The Kuznets curve and the great U-turn: Income inequality in US counties, 1970 to 1990. American Sociological Review. 1997; **62**(February):12-33

[11] Khan S, Yahong W, Zeeshan A. Impact of poverty and income inequality on the ecological footprint in Asian developing economies: Assessment of sustainable development goals. Energy Reports. 2022;**8**:670-679

[12] Le TH, Chang Y, Park D. Renewable and nonrenewable energy consumption, economic growth, and emissions: International evidence. The Energy Journal. 2020a;**41**(2):73-92

[13] Le TH, Nguyen CP, Su TD, Tran-Nam B. The Kuznets curve for export diversification and income inequality: Evidence from a global sample. Economic Analysis and Policy. 2020b;**65**: 21-39

[14] Shahbaz M, Solarin SA, Ozturk I. Environmental Kuznets curve hypothesis and the role of globalization in selected African countries. Ecological Indicators. 2016;**67**:623-636

[15] Farhani S, Ozturk I. Causal relationship between CO 2 emissions, real GDP, energy consumption, financial development, trade openness, and urbanization in Tunisia. Environmental Science and Pollution Research. 2015;**22** (20):15663-15676

[16] Uzar U, Eyuboglu K. The nexus between income inequality and CO2 emissions in Turkey. Journal of Cleaner Production. 2019;**227**:149-157

[17] Baek J, Gweisah G. Does income inequality harm the environment?: Empirical evidence from the United States. Energy Policy. 2013;**62**:1434-1437

[18] Kasuga H, Takaya M. Does inequality affect environmental quality? Evidence from major Japanese cities. Journal of Cleaner Production. 2017;**142**: 3689-3701

[19] Wan G, Wang C, Wang J, Zhang X. The income inequality-CO2 emissions nexus: Transmission mechanisms. Ecological Economics. 2022;**195**:107360

[20] Demir C, Cergibozan R, Gök A. Income inequality and CO2 emissions: Empirical evidence from Turkey. Energy & Environment. 2019;**30**(3):444-461

[21] Uddin MM, Mishra V, Smyth R. Income inequality and CO2 emissions in the G7, 1870–2014: Evidence from non-parametric modelling. Energy Economics. 2020;**88**:104780

[22] Belaïd F, Boubaker S, Kafrouni R. Carbon emissions, income inequality and environmental degradation: The case of Mediterranean countries. The European Journal of Comparative Economics. 2020;**17**(1):73-102

[23] Halkos GE, Paizanos EA. The effect of government expenditure on the environment: An empirical investigation. Ecological Economics. 2013;**91**:48-56

[24] López R, Galinato GI, Islam A. Fiscal spending and the environment: Theory and empirics. Journal of Environmental Economics and Management. 2011;**62** (2):180-198

[25] Bajo-Rubio O. A further generalization of the Solow growth model: The role of the public sector. Economics Letters. 2000;**68**(1):79-84

[26] Bergh A, Karlsson M. Government size and growth: Accounting for economic freedom and globalization. Public Choice. 2010;**142**(1):195-213

[27] Bernauer T, Koubi V. States as providers of public goods: How does government size affect environmental quality?. 2006

[28] Carlsson F, Lundström S. Economic freedom and growth: Decomposing the effects. Public Choice. 2002;**112**(3):335-344

[29] Grossman GM, Krueger AB. The inverted-U: What does it mean? Environment and Development Economics. 1996;**1**(1):119-122

[30] Stiglitz JE. Inequality and environmental policy. In: Dabelko GD, Conca K, editors. Green Planet Blues: Critical Perspectives on Global Environmental Politics. Routledge. New York, USA: Informa Group; 2014, 2019

[31] Kempf H, Rossignol S. Is inequality harmful for the environment in a growing economy? Economics and Politics. 2007;**19**(1):53-71

[32] Ridzuan S. Inequality and the environmental Kuznets curve. Journal of Cleaner Production. 2019;**228**:1472-1481

[33] Franzen A, Meyer R. Environmental attitudes in cross-national perspective: A multilevel analysis of the ISSP 1993 and 2000. European Sociological Review. 2010;**26**(2):219-234

[34] Facchini F, Gaeta GL, Michallet B. Who cares about the environment? An

empirical analysis of the evolution of political parties' environmental concern in European countries (1970–2008). Land Use Policy. 2017;**64**:200-211

[35] Magnani E. The Environmental Kuznets curve, environmental protection policy and income distribution. Ecological Economics. 2000;**32**(3):431-443

[36] Blundell R, Bond S. Initial conditions and moment restrictions in dynamic panel data models. Journal of Econometrics. 1998;**87**(1):115-143

[37] Fukase E. Revisiting linkages between openness, education and economic growth: System GMM approach. Journal of Economic Integration. March 2010;**25**(1):194-223

[38] United Nations. Country classification. World situation and prospects (WESP). Statistical Annex. 2020

[39] Solt F. The standardized world income inequality database. Social Science Quarterly. 2016;**97**(5):1267-1281

[40] Solt F. Measuring income inequality across countries and over time: The standardized world income inequality database. Social Science Quarterly. 2020; **101**(3):1183-1199

[41] Choi G. Revisiting the redistribution hypothesis with perceived inequality and redistributive preferences. European Journal of Political Economy. 2019;**58**: 220-244

[42] Uzar U. Is income inequality a driver for renewable energy consumption? Journal of Cleaner Production. 2020;**255**: 120287

Chapter 2

Investors' Greed and Fear: An Event Study of Analyst Recommendations

Qingxia (Jenny) Wang

Abstract

We investigate the effect of the skewness developed by the CBOE, called SKEW, on investors' reactions to analyst recommendations. Our results show that the abnormal stock returns around analyst recommendation revisions are closely correlated with contemporaneous SKEW changes. Specifically, positive (negative) abnormal returns following analyst recommendation upgrades (downgrades) are stronger when daily SKEW increases (decreases). A potential explanation for this relation is that SKEW captures investors' greed (excitement) in the stock market. Similar to the CBOE VIX, SKEW might act as another measure to reflect investors' moods or sentiments. However, in contrast to VIX, which is usually used as investors' fear gauge, SKEW is the opposite of investors' fear, measuring investors' consensus view of future positive news. Furthermore, we show that the magnitudes of abnormal returns associated with the change in SKEW are larger for the NASDAQ than for the NYSE on recommendation announcement days. This may manifest the different types of firms listed on these two stock exchanges.

Keywords: analyst recommendation revision, abnormal return, investors' greed, investors' fear, SKEW, VIX

1. Introduction

Prior literature has extensively investigated the market volatility expectations, captured by the implied volatility index (VIX).[1] VIX is developed by the Chicago Board Options Exchange (CBOE), measuring investors' fear in the US stock market [1, 2]. Later, the CBOE developed another index, SKEW, to estimate the tail risk of the S&P 500 returns that are not fully captured by VIX. While empirical evidence documents that asymmetry measures outperform volatility measures in predicting market returns, studies on SKEW are scant and it is inconclusive on whether SKEW could be a fear or greed indicator. Using a similar procedure for constructing the CBOE SKEW, Elyasiani et al. [7] propose an Italian SKEW (ITSKEW). They argue that SKEW (CBOE SKEW or ITSKEW) acts as a measure of market greed (excitement), and has a

[1] For example, see [1–6].

significant contemporaneous relation with returns.[2] However, Mora-Valencia et al. [8] explain the SKEW index as a fear indicator. Liu and Faff [9] question the usefulness of SKEW as an indicator of institutional anxiety. Our study complements prior research by further examining the effect of SKEW on stock returns around corporate events. Specifically, we investigate how the change in SKEW around analyst recommendations is related to announcement returns.

Analyst recommendation revisions contain useful information for investment decisions. For example, Stickel [10] shows that brokerage analyst recommendations have a strong effect on short-term stock prices. Womack [11] provides evidence that there exist significant discrepancies between pre-recommendation prices and post-recommendation values. Barber et al. [12] document that investors can earn abnormal returns, both gross and net of trading costs, by taking advantage of analyst recommendations. Jegadeesh and Kim [13] provide international evidence from G7 countries to show that stock prices react significantly to analyst recommendation revisions. Jegadeesh and Kim [14] further document a stronger market reaction to recommendation revisions when the new recommendations move away from the consensus. Loh and Stulz [15] show that in bad times, recommendation revisions have a larger impact on stock prices.

In general, the literature finds that around analyst recommendations, upgrades are related to higher abnormal stock returns, whereas downgrades are associated with lower abnormal stock returns (normally negative abnormal stock returns). Based on stocks listed on the NYSE, Kliger and Kudryavtsev [16] explore the interaction between abnormal stock returns and volatility expectations around recommendation revisions. They use the CBOE VIX to capture investors' market volatility expectations, which is also known as the investors' fear gauge [1, 2]. Their results show that VIX changes are highly correlated with investors' sentiment by reporting that positive (negative) abnormal stock returns are stronger when the daily VIX decreases (increases) for recommendation upgrades (downgrades). In the spirit of Kliger and Kudryavtsev [16], we examine the effect of SKEW on investors' reaction to analyst recommendation revisions. Skewness demonstrates one type of behavior regarding investors' attitude toward risks. For example, Han [17] shows that model-free implied skewness (MFIS) is associated with investor sentiment in which several investor sentiment proxies are applied [18–20]. Green and Hwang [21] document that initial public offerings (IPOs) with high expected skewness achieve greater first-day returns. This might be explained as individuals' affinity for lotteries, reflected by higher skewness.

We examine stocks listed on the NYSE and the NASDAQ separately because, on these two stock exchanges, the types of listed firms and investors are potentially different [22–25] and the market responses to news announcements are also different [26, 27].[3] We further contrast the effect of the market SKEW on investors' responses to analyst recommendation revisions on these two stock exchanges.

For both the NYSE and the NASDAQ, we show that the abnormal returns before announcement days (day −1) and on the announcement days (day 0) are significantly higher when SKEW increases (i.e., ΔSKEW>0) than when SKEW

[2] For instance, the change in SKEW during time *t* is significantly related to stock returns during the same period.

[3] Investors might have a different perception of stocks listed on the NYSE and NASDAQ. For example, most firms that trade on the NASDAQ are the young, high technology, and innovative firms.

decreases (i.e., $\Delta SKEW < 0$). For recommendation upgrades, the abnormal returns for these 2 days are generally positive[4] and are larger for $\Delta SKEW > 0$ than for $\Delta SKEW < 0$. Accordingly, for recommendation downgrades, the abnormal returns for these 2 days are generally negative[5]. Moreover, the magnitudes of abnormal returns for $\Delta SKEW > 0$ are significantly less than that for $\Delta SKEW < 0$. That is, abnormal returns are more negative on both days when SKEW decreases than SKEW increases. We argue that these results are analogous to investors' preference for stocks with lottery features [20, 28].

Furthermore, we show that on recommendation revision days (i.e., day 0), the magnitudes of corresponding abnormal returns are larger for stocks listed on the NASDAQ than those listed on the NYSE, that is, abnormal returns are more positive (negative) for upgrades (downgrades). This could be explained by the high volatility of high-tech stocks listed on the NASDAQ, which contributes to higher (lower) abnormal returns for upgrades (downgrades).

Overall, we observe a positive relationship between the changes in SKEW and abnormal returns around recommendation revisions. As such, we propose that SKEW is an indicator of investors' greed measure rather than a fear gauge. This is consistent with the study of Green and Hwang [21] and Elyasiani et al. [7].

Our study contributes to the literature on psychological bias and investors' decision-making in financial markets around news announcements. Through the corporate news events (i.e., analyst recommendations), we show that the CBOE SKEW index is useful in proxying investor sentiment. Investors prefer a higher skewness index, which represents greater investors' greed. These results are observed from stocks listed on both the NYSE and the NASDAQ. Moreover, investors might capture higher abnormal returns around recommendation upgrades and lose more around recommendation downgrades from stocks listed on the NASDAQ than those listed on the NYSE. In summary, this study provides significant implications for investors when making their investment decisions around news events in different stock exchanges.

The remainder of this paper proceeds as follows. Section 2 describes the data sample and reports the descriptive statistics. Section 3 presents the empirical results, and Section 4 concludes.

2. Data and descriptive statistics

We focus on analyst recommendation revisions for the NYSE-listed and NASDAQ-listed companies, from January 2002 to December 2019. We collect data from several data sources. Analyst recommendation data are from the Institutional Brokers' Estimate System (I/B/E/S) through the Wharton Research Data System (WRDS). I/B/E/S ranks recommendations from 1 (strong buy) to 5 (sell)[6]. For ease of interpretation, we

---

[4] The abnormal return is only negative and with a small magnitude on day −1 for $\Delta SKEW < 0$. Taking the NYSE for example, the magnitude of abnormal return for $\Delta SKEW > 0$ is 0.60%, but it is only 0.13% for $\Delta SKEW < 0$ (roughly one-fifth of that for $\Delta SKEW > 0$).

[5] Except for a smaller negative return on day −1 for $\Delta SKEW > 0$, the explanation for this is similar to that in footnote 3.

[6] Specifically, analyst recommendations in I/B/E/S are ranked as: 1 = Strong buy, 2 = Buy, 3 = Hold, 4 = Underperform, 5 = Sell.

follow Howe. et al. [29] and Loh and Stulz [30] and reverse the recommendation ratings so that the highest (lowest) rating represents the most (least) favorable recommendation. After reversing, we have 1 = Sell, 2 = Underperform, 3 = Hold, 4 = Buy and 5 = Strong buy.[7] We require any analyst recommendation to have a CUSIP number and a recommendation date.

We analyze revisions, rather than levels, in analyst recommendations. This is because Jegadeesh et al. [31] find that recommendation levels provide little incremental investment value relative to other investment signals, and Jegadeesh and Kim [14] show that recommendation changes are more informative than levels in predicting stock returns. We follow Loh and Stulz [30] and calculate the difference between current and prior ratings made by the same analyst. As recommendation levels range from 1 (sell) to 5 (strong buy), recommendation revisions range from −4 to +4. We define the recommendation revision with a positive (negative) value as an upgrade (downgrade). We omit zero recommendation revisions because zero changes suggest that the analysts possess no incremental new information. We also follow Barber et al. [32] and remove outdated observations whose prior recommendation exceeds 1 year. When multiple analysts issue recommendations for one stock within one trading day, we average all of the recommendation revisions. If the average value of recommendation revisions is positive (negative), we define it as an upgrade (downgrade) [33].

We collect stock prices from the Center for Research in Security Prices (CRSP) database. To be included in our sample, the stock must have a CUSIP number and have at least 251 trading days before, and 10 days after the corresponding recommendation revisions. The absolute daily historical stock return should not exceed 65% [16]. We identify stocks listed on the NYSE and the NASDAQ using the stock exchange code (EXCHCD). The NYSE-listed stock has an EXCHCD of 1 and the NASDAQ-listed stock has an EXCHCD of 3. The NYSE and the NASDAQ index prices are extracted from www.finance.yahoo.com. SKEW and VIX data are obtained from the CBOE website.[8]

Table 1 reports the yearly descriptive summary for the stocks listed on the NYSE (Panel A) and the NASDAQ (Panel B). The market capitalization (MarketCap) is computed as the share price multiplied by the total shares outstanding on the event day. The stock's market model beta is estimated over an estimate window [−251, −31] prior to the recommendation revision. For the NYSE, the MarketCap ranges from $1 to $461,021 million with a standard deviation of $31,130 million. The market model beta varies from −1.359 to 5.818 and the standard deviation is 0.486. The daily historical return ranges from −0.632% to 0.621%, with a standard deviation of 0.056%. We observe a very low mean and high standard deviation of stock returns in 2002 and around 2008 and 2009. It is very clear that the year 2008–2009 is related to the global financial crisis, but the year 2002 might be affected by the NASDAQ "bubble." [34] Accordingly, we observe a higher market model beta with a value of 1.21 in 2009 and 1.24 in 2016.

---

[7] "Underperform" is a type of stock trading recommendation between "Sell" and "Hold". Clearly, analysts recommend that a stock's performance is below the average market performance. In different databases or analyst ranking systems, different terms may be used. For example, "Strong sell" and "Sell" would be used rather than "Sell" and "Underperform".

[8] https://www.cboe.com/us/indices/dashboard/skew/
http://www.cboe.com/products/vix-index-volatility/vix-options-and-futures/vix-index/vix-historical-data.

Year	Number of Rec. revisions	MarketCap ($ millions)				Market model beta				Historical returns (%)			
		Mean	Std.	Min	Max	Mean	Std.	Min	Max	Mean	Std.	Min	Max
Panel A: NYSE													
2002	1841	11,412	26,932	1	297,139	1.010	0.555	−1.359	3.179	−0.009	0.072	−0.632	0.317
2003	2644	10,566	24,951	2	263,281	0.949	0.486	−0.407	3.001	0.000	0.049	−0.495	0.325
2004	2352	10,899	27,341	11	377,531	1.040	0.494	−0.272	4.064	−0.001	0.043	−0.341	0.231
2005	1990	12,389	30,657	2	407,438	1.173	0.451	−0.005	3.360	0.000	0.052	−0.568	0.360
2006	1892	12,434	27,143	14	399,501	1.101	0.465	0.034	2.998	0.000	0.047	−0.371	0.468
2007	2367	13,032	28,599	3	432,187	1.110	0.433	−0.063	2.604	−0.002	0.052	−0.630	0.547
2008	2971	12,390	26,933	4	461,021	1.127	0.406	0.045	3.108	−0.009	0.078	−0.627	0.512
2009	2752	9729	24,858	13	391,672	1.206	0.445	0.053	3.381	0.006	0.065	−0.475	0.568
2010	2158	12,043	26,594	14	316,848	1.169	0.490	0.008	3.052	0.001	0.045	−0.335	0.571
2011	2519	14,380	31,510	20	403,397	1.101	0.387	−0.248	2.506	0.005	0.047	−0.286	0.589
2012	2287	13,956	30,307	16	407,762	1.173	0.439	0.099	3.020	−0.001	0.048	−0.628	0.344
2013	1725	14,025	28,069	17	411,208	1.122	0.437	−0.028	3.251	0.001	0.047	−0.281	0.524
2014	1576	16,078	31,959	1	415,876	1.076	0.409	−0.102	3.177	0.000	0.045	−0.481	0.298
2015	1583	15,969	36,477	1	363,847	1.134	0.498	−0.179	3.778	−0.001	0.056	−0.535	0.439
2016	1768	16,176	36,698	15	340,695	1.242	0.585	−0.373	5.818	−0.002	0.063	−0.509	0.559
2017	1483	18,418	39,719	17	355,281	1.380	0.675	−0.241	4.905	−0.001	0.054	−0.352	0.621
2018	1264	22,934	49,778	20	401,343	1.107	0.497	−0.327	3.267	−0.001	0.053	−0.444	0.403
2019	1339	18,576	40,818	5	421,857	1.169	0.512	−0.609	3.102	−0.003	0.064	−0.572	0.448
Total	36,511	13,582	31,130	1	461,021	1.127	0.486	−1.359	5.818	−0.001	0.056	−0.632	0.621
Upgrades	18,124	13,859	30,439	1	461,021	1.132	0.489	−1.359	5.818	0.019	0.046	−0.630	0.589
Downgrades	18,387	13,310	31,795	1	422,622	1.121	0.482	−1.119	3.855	−0.020	0.058	−0.632	0.621

Year	Number of Rec. revisions	MarketCap ($ millions)				Market model beta				Historical returns (%)			
		Mean	Std.	Min	Max	Mean	Std.	Min	Max	Mean	Std.	Min	Max
Panel B: NASDAQ													
2002	1440	5029	21,513	3	293,626	0.859	0.577	−0.344	2.388	−0.014	0.095	−0.602	0.526
2003	2038	4217	19,361	4	288,100	0.877	0.527	−0.394	2.365	0.003	0.080	−0.646	0.594
2004	1896	5442	19,885	4	306,461	1.017	0.521	−0.290	3.017	−0.004	0.072	−0.408	0.537
2005	1886	4408	17,814	6	294,645	1.064	0.513	−0.183	2.673	−0.003	0.078	−0.635	0.520
2006	1928	4491	16,759	15	275,384	1.070	0.454	−0.356	2.517	0.002	0.078	−0.620	0.513
2007	1677	4442	16,696	7	304,443	1.079	0.430	−0.337	2.514	−0.001	0.082	−0.643	0.630
2008	2053	4903	18,223	3	297,172	1.004	0.367	−0.354	2.405	−0.011	0.101	−0.636	0.639
2009	2078	4233	15,793	5	210,114	1.098	0.378	−0.197	2.439	0.005	0.081	−0.612	0.484
2010	1705	6102	23,380	16	283,897	1.167	0.430	−0.040	2.684	0.001	0.065	−0.462	0.541
2011	1847	6386	19,960	11	369,044	1.141	0.376	−0.555	2.539	−0.001	0.074	−0.525	0.561
2012	1482	7758	39,746	12	654,966	1.204	0.378	0.005	2.624	−0.002	0.080	−0.498	0.545
2013	1086	10,172	39,767	23	464,875	1.053	0.350	0.048	2.212	0.001	0.087	−0.645	0.644
2014	949	11,372	46,923	19	604,775	1.118	0.448	−0.219	2.981	−0.002	0.086	−0.616	0.619
2015	1019	10,742	46,159	12	731,588	1.035	0.382	−0.237	2.598	0.002	0.090	−0.461	0.621
2016	1000	13,189	59,554	32	614,229	1.009	0.384	−0.339	2.591	−0.004	0.089	−0.616	0.590
2017	924	11,670	37,359	33	674,338	1.108	0.475	−0.236	2.941	−0.001	0.080	−0.541	0.615
2018	832	15,698	57,970	15	973,230	0.895	0.459	−0.575	2.484	0.000	0.087	−0.641	0.519
2019	959	23,537	90,062	4	1,105,306	0.940	0.419	−0.371	2.142	−0.004	0.090	−0.649	0.545
Total	26,799	7296	33,942	3	1,105,306	1.044	0.454	−0.575	3.017	−0.002	0.083	−0.649	0.644
Upgrades	13,055	7741	33,913	3	1,105,306	1.058	0.454	−0.575	2.981	0.033	0.065	−0.610	0.644
Downgrades	13,744	6873	33,965	3	973,230	1.032	0.455	−0.555	3.017	−0.034	0.085	−0.649	−0.630

Table 1.
Yearly sample descriptive statistics for stocks listed on the NYSE (Panel A) and the NASDAQ (Panel B).

For the NASDAQ, the MarketCap varies from \$3 to \$1,105,306 million with a standard deviation of \$33,942 million. The maximum MarketCap appears in 2019, which shows a large value increase in high-tech stocks in recent years. Interestingly, we observe a higher average market model beta with a value of 1.20 in 2012 rather than in the 2009 financial crisis period. The daily historical return ranges from −0.649% to 0.644%, with a standard deviation of 0.083%. It shows that the stock return is more volatile for the stocks listed on the NASDAQ. Similar to the NYSE, a very low mean and high standard deviation of stock returns are observed in 2002 and around 2008 and 2009. Pástor and Veronesi [34] show the NASDAQ "bubble" in the late 1990s, with the NASDAQ index price varying significantly from 5048 in March 2000 to 1114 in October 2002. This was accompanied by high return volatility, which is around 10%.

3. Empirical results

In this section, we present our empirical results for the NYSE and the NASDAQ. We define the analyst recommendation revision date as day 0. We begin the empirical analysis by investigating the daily abnormal return (AR) over the event window surrounding the analyst recommendation revision. We use the market model to calculate AR_i [16]:

$$R_{i,t} = \alpha_i + \beta_i R_{m,t} + \varepsilon_{i,t}, \tag{1}$$

where $R_{i,t}$ is the daily return for stock i on date t, and $R_{m,t}$ is the market return. α_i and β_i are the corresponding regression coefficients, and $\varepsilon_{i,t}$ is the error term. We use the NYSE composite index return and the NASDAQ composite index return as the market returns, respectively. We estimate Eq. (1) using an estimation window that covers day −251 to day −30. Following Savor [35], we calculate the abnormal return $AR_{i,t}$ as:

$$AR_{i,t} = R_{i,t} - \hat{\beta}_i R_{m,t}, \tag{2}$$

where $\hat{\beta}_i$ is the estimated coefficient of market returns in Eq. (1).

Table 2 reports the average daily stock ARs for upgrades and downgrades over the [−10,+10] event window.[9] Panel A and Panel B are for the NYSE and NASDAQ, respectively. For visualization, we take the NYSE for example to plot the average ARs for downgrades (Panel A) and upgrades (Panel B) over this event window. **Figure 1** shows the plots.

For both the NYSE and the NASDAQ, we observe that abnormal stock returns increase (decrease) considerably on the day of recommendation upwards (downwards), that is, day 0 (or event day), with some abnormal behavior on day −1. This tendency reflects analysts' perspectives on stocks' performance - upgraded (downgraded) stocks might be underestimated (overestimated) after experiencing a period of negative (positive) ARs [16].

[9] We also calculate ARs for the event window [−30,+10] and obtain qualitatively similar results, which are available upon request.

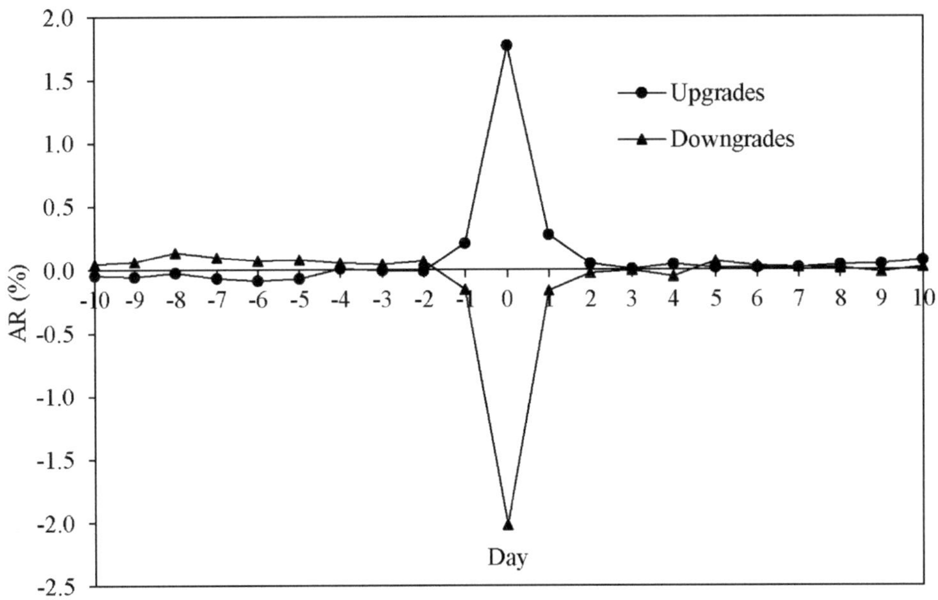

Figure 1.
Abnormal stock returns over the event window. This figure plots the abnormal stock returns over the [−10,+10] event window surrounding analyst recommendation revisions for the stocks listed on the NYSE.

Event window [−10,+10]	**Upgrades**		**Downgrades**	
	Average AR (%)	***t*-statistics**	**Average AR (%)**	***t*-statistics**
Panel A: NYSE				
−10	−0.05	−2.48	0.05	2.28
−9	−0.06	−2.93	0.06	3.28
−8	−0.02	−1.22	0.14	6.84
−7	−0.07	−3.50	0.10	5.21
−6	−0.09	−4.70	0.07	3.67
−5	−0.07	−3.65	0.08	3.86
−4	0.01	0.34	0.05	2.80
−3	−0.01	−0.33	0.04	1.98
−2	−0.01	−0.53	0.07	2.83
−1	0.21	7.36	−0.16	−4.25
0	1.77	55.80	−2.02	−49.19
1	0.28	13.78	−0.17	−7.76
2	0.05	2.67	−0.03	−1.27
3	0.01	0.30	0.00	−0.27
4	0.04	2.28	−0.05	−2.81
5	0.01	0.70	0.07	2.96
6	0.01	0.71	0.03	1.34
7	0.02	0.98	0.02	0.99
8	0.04	2.29	0.01	0.70
9	0.04	2.42	−0.02	−0.82
10	0.08	3.92	0.02	1.01
Panel B: NASDAQ				
−10	−0.07	−2.31	0.09	2.60
−9	−0.09	−3.69	0.04	1.70
−8	−0.07	−2.74	0.13	4.50
−7	−0.11	−4.43	0.15	5.54

Event window [−10,+10]	Upgrades		Downgrades	
	Average AR (%)	*t*-statistics	Average AR (%)	*t*-statistics
−6	−0.10	−3.51	0.14	4.82
−5	−0.16	−5.05	0.10	3.47
−4	−0.09	−3.31	0.11	3.77
−3	−0.05	−1.45	0.11	3.51
−2	-0.05	−1.68	0.18	4.63
−1	0.12	2.60	−0.12	−2.20
0	3.17	57.26	−3.47	−48.94
1	0.28	9.89	−0.22	−7.35
2	0.09	3.54	−0.10	−3.63
3	0.05	2.04	−0.08	−2.75
4	0.04	1.44	−0.05	−2.05
5	0.07	2.54	−0.01	−0.44
6	0.04	1.67	0.06	2.23
7	−0.02	−0.64	0.03	1.16
8	0.03	1.05	−0.01	−0.36
9	0.02	0.75	−0.04	−1.51
10	0.00	−0.13	0.00	0.16

Table 2.
The abnormal returns (ARs) around analyst recommendation revisions for the NYSE (Panel A) and the NASDAQ (Panel B).

Furthermore, we find that the corresponding increase or decrease of abnormal returns around recommendation revisions is larger for the NASDAQ than for the NYSE. Specifically, on day 0, the average abnormal return of upgrades (downgrades) is 3.17% (−3.47%) for the NASDAQ and 1.77% (−2.02%) for the NYSE. This suggests the potential difference of stocks and investor perspectives on these stocks between the NYSE and the NASDAQ. The firms listed on the NASDAQ are generally small and young, and accordingly, their share prices are highly volatile. For example, the mean of the MarketCap for stocks listed on the NASDAQ is $7296 million, much smaller than the mean of the MarketCap of $13,582 million for stocks listed on the NYSE. The average standard deviation of historical returns for stocks listed on the NASDAQ (0.083%) is higher than that for stocks listed on the NYSE (0.056%).

3.1 The effect of SKEW

Similar to Kliger and Kudryavtsev [16], we document a significant relationship between abnormal returns around recommendation revisions and contemporaneous SKEW changes (ΔSKEW). To compare with Kliger and Kudryavtsev [16], we also present the results concerning VIX in the next subsection.

3.1.1 The effect on day −1 and day 0

Table 3 reports the effect of SKEW on investors' reaction to analyst recommendation revisions on days −1 and 0.

Panels A and B present the results for the NYSE and the NASDAQ, respectively. ΔSKEW is the change of SKEW corresponding to day t for stock i's recommendation revisions. We show that the contemporaneous SKEW changes have a statistically significant effect on the abnormal returns around recommendation revisions. An increase (decrease) in SKEW is related to a larger (smaller) average AR for both

Type of recommendation revision	Average AR on day −1 (%)			Average AR on day 0 (%)		
	ΔSKEW > 0	ΔSKEW < 0	Diff (t-statistic)	ΔSKEW > 0	ΔSKEW < 0	Diff (t-statistic)
Panel A: NYSE						
Upgrades	0.60	−0.13	0.73*** (11.48)	2.25	1.52	0.73*** (10.67)
Downgrades	0.19	−0.43	0.62*** (8.02)	−1.70	−2.34	0.64*** (7.52)
Panel B: NASDAQ						
Upgrades	0.48	−0.19	0.67*** (7.15)	3.56	2.97	0.59*** (5.14)
Downgrades	0.29	−0.39	0.68*** (6.03)	−2.97	−3.90	0.93*** (6.43)

*Note: *, ** and *** denote significance levels at 10%, 5%, and 1%, respectively.*

Table 3.
The effect of contemporaneous daily changes in SKEW on the abnormal returns (ARs) around event days for the NYSE (Panel A) and the NASDAQ (Panel B).

upgrades and downgrades compared with the unconditional AR (see **Table 2**). Take the NYSE for example. For ΔSKEW > 0, the average AR on day −1 is 0.60% (0.19%) for upgrades (downgrades), however, for ΔSKEW < 0, it is −0.13% (−0.43%). The difference of the average AR between ΔSKEW > 0 and ΔSKEW < 0 is statistically significant, with a value of 0.73% (*t*-statistic = 11.48) for upgrades and 0.62% (*t*-statistic = 8.02) for downgrades.

On day 0, the corresponding average AR become more positive (negative) for upgrades (downgrades), manifested by the results shown in **Table 2**. Specifically, for ΔSKEW > 0, the average AR is 2.25% (−1.70%) for upgrades (downgrades); forΔSKEW < 0, it becomes 1.52% (−2.34%). The findings indicate that abnormal returns around analyst recommendation revisions are closely associated with contemporaneous SKEW changes. That is, positive events (upgrades) drive significantly higher ARs captured by the daily SKEW increase (i.e., a higher expectation of earnings, or greed), and negative events (downgrades) drive significantly lower ARs captured by the daily SKEW decrease (i.e., a lower expectation of earnings).

For the NASDAQ, the results are generally consistent with those for the NYSE. Interestingly, on day −1, we find that the magnitudes of average ARs for all cases (upgrades and downgrades, ΔSKEW > 0 and ΔSKEW < 0) are generally close to corresponding results of the NYSE. For example, for upgrades and ΔSKEW > 0, the average AR is 0.48% for the NASDAQ and 0.60% for the NYSE, with a difference of 0.12%. However, on day 0, the average ARs' corresponding magnitudes are larger for the NASDAQ than for the NYSE. Again, for upgrades and ΔSKEW > 0, the average AR is 2.25% for the NASDAQ and 3.56% for the NYSE, with a difference of 1.31%, almost ten times of that on day −1. On the one hand, this implies that SKEW is more informative on the event day than the day before. On the other hand, the findings indicate that recommendation revision may have a stronger effect on stocks listed on the NASDAQ than those listed on the NYSE. This is probably explained by the potential difference in the types of listing firms and the ways how investors perceive the firms. The NASDAQ is typically a high-tech market, the NASDAQ-listed firms are mainly technology, young and fast-growing firms. The stocks listed on the NASDAQ are considered to be more volatile (or say highly uncertain), and accordingly, investors demand a higher return [34]. Correspondingly, this high volatility (uncertainty) contributes to higher abnormal returns for recommendation upgrades but more negative abnormal returns for recommendation downgrades.

3.1.2 The effect on the cumulative days (−1,0)

Now we look at the effect of the changes in SKEW on the cumulative abnormal returns (i.e., CARs) over days −1 and 0. **Table 4** reports the results for both the NYSE (Panel A) and the NASDAQ (Panel B). Cumulative ΔSKEW represents the contemporaneous cumulative changes in SKEW over days −1 and 0. We present further evidence that SKEW has a statistical and economic effect on stock returns around analyst recommendations. That is, we find similar return patterns for Cumulative ΔSKEW to those on separated single days (i.e., day −1 and day 0). Taking the NYSE for example, for upgrades, the significantly *positive* difference (i.e., Diff = 0.83% with t-statistic = 8.93) indicates that the CAR (with a value of 2.53%) is stronger when the cumulative change in SKEW is *positive* (i.e., Cumulative ΔSKEW > 0) than that (with a value of 1.70%) when the cumulative change in SKEW is *negative* (i.e., Cumulative ΔSKEW < 0). For downgrades, the significantly *positive* difference (i.e., Diff = 0.57% with t-statistic = 4.89) also indicates that the CAR (with a value of −1.87%) is stronger when the cumulative change in SKEW is *positive* (i.e., Cumulative ΔSKEW > 0) than that (with a value of −2.45%) when the cumulative change in SKEW is *negative* (i.e., Cumulative ΔSKEW < 0).

Next, we find that the corresponding magnitudes of the CARs are larger for the NASDAQ than the NYSE. In summary, these results provide further evidence supporting the hypothesis that abnormal returns around analyst recommendation revisions are closely correlated with contemporaneous changes in SKEW.

3.1.3 Additional tests

To further validate the event results obtained in Section 3.1, we apply a simple regression model (i.e., univariate model) to test whether SKEW could act as one measure of investors' greed or fear. We write the regression model as [7]:

$$AR_{i,t} = \alpha + \beta \Delta \mathrm{SKEW}_t + \varepsilon_{i,t}, \tag{3}$$

In the regression analysis, we take day 0 for example and present the results in **Table 5**. From Panel A, we observe that the regression coefficient on the changes in SKEW (i.e., ΔSKEW) is positive and significant, with a value of 0.11 (t-statistic = 9.81) for upgrades and 0.09 (t-statistic = 5.85) for downgrades. These results suggest that an

Type of recommendation revision	**CAR over days −1 and 0 (%)**		
	Cumulative $\Delta SKEW > 0$	**Cumulative $\Delta SKEW < 0$**	**Diff (t-statistic)**
Panel A: NYSE			
Upgrades	2.53	1.70	0.83*** (8.93)
Downgrades	−1.87	−2.45	0.57*** (4.89)
Panel B: NASDAQ			
Upgrades	3.76	3.06	0.70*** (4.79)
Downgrades	−3.04	−3.94	0.90*** (4.89)

*Note: *, ** and *** denote significance levels at 10%, 5%, and 1%, respectively.*

Table 4.
The effect of changes in SKEW on the cumulative abnormal returns (CARs) for the NYSE (Panel A) and the NASDAQ (Panel B).

	Upgrades	Downgrades
Panel A:		
ΔSKEW	0.11*** (9.81)	0.09*** (5.85)
Intercept	1.88*** (55.0)	−2.03*** (−47.50)
Panel B:		
$\Delta SKEW^{+}$	0.10*** (5.31)	0.05* (1.88)
$\Delta SKEW^{-}$	0.13*** (6.17)	0.13*** (5.01)
Intercept	1.91*** (40.0)	−1.95*** (−33.08)

*Note: The numbers in parentheses are t-statistics. *, ** and *** denote significance levels at 10%, 5%, and 1%, respectively.*

Table 5.
Regression results for the abnormal returns (ARs) and the changes in SKEW (ΔSKEW) on recommendation revision days.

increase in SKEW is associated with an increase in abnormal returns regardless of recommendation upgrades or downgrades. Consistent with the event results presented in Sections 3.1.1 and 3.1.2, we argue that SKEW should be a proper measure of investors' greed.

We also examine the effect of positive and negative changes in SKEW on stock abnormal returns by separatingΔSKEW into the positive part (i.e., $\Delta SKEW^{+}$) and the negative part (i.e., $\Delta SKEW^{-}$). We estimate the following regression:

$$AR_{i,t} = \alpha + \beta_1 \Delta SKEW_t^{+} + \beta_2 \Delta SKEW_t^{-} + \varepsilon_t, \qquad (4)$$

where $\Delta SKEW^{+}$ and $\Delta SKEW^{+}$ are defined as:
$\Delta SKEW_t^{+} = \Delta SKEW_t$, if $\Delta SKEW_t > 0$; otherwise $\Delta SKEW_t^{+} = 0$, and
$\Delta SKEW_t^{-} = \Delta SKEW_t$, if $\Delta SKEW_t < 0$; otherwise $\Delta SKEW_t^{-} = 0$.

Panel B in **Table 5** reports the results. Again, regardless of upgrades or downgrades, we observe positive and significant estimated coefficients on both $\Delta SKEW^{+}$ and $\Delta SKEW^{-}$. We also use Eqs. (3) and (4) to test the effect of changes in SKEW on the day prior to recommendation revisions (i.e., day −1), and obtain qualitatively similar results.[10] In summary, these results provide further evidence that SKEW could be considered as an investors' greed indicator.

3.2 The effect of VIX[11]

3.2.1 The effect on day −1 and day 0

To make a comparison with VIX, we test the relationship between changes in VIX (ΔVIX) and abnormal returns around recommendation revisions. Kliger and Kudryavtsev [16] only examine stocks listed on the NYSE. We extend our tests to stocks listed on the NASDAQ as well. **Table 6** reports the results on days −1 and 0.

Panels A and B present the results for the NYSE and the NASDAQ, respectively. ΔVIX is the change of VIX price corresponding to day t for stock i's recommendation revisions. Consistent with the findings of Kliger and Kudryavtsev [16], the

[10] The results are not reported but are available upon request.

[11] The effect of VIX is examined in [16], which only includes firms listed on the NYSE. The purpose of Section 3.2 has twofold. First, we compare the different effects of SKEW and VIX. Second, we extend the test in [16] and compare the effect of VIX on firms listed on the NYSE and those listed on the NASDAQ.

Type of recommendation revision	Average AR on day −1 (%)			Average AR on day 0 (%)		
	$\Delta VIX > 0$	$\Delta VIX < 0$	Diff (t-statistic)	$\Delta VIX > 0$	$\Delta VIX < 0$	Diff (t-statistic)
Panel A: NYSE						
Upgrades	−0.76	1.17	−1.93*** (−31.12)	0.84	2.67	−1.83*** (−26.80)
Downgrades	−0.96	0.70	−1.66*** (−21.63)	−2.97	−1.25	−1.72*** (−20.34)
Panel B: NASDAQ						
Upgrades	−0.80	1.05	−1.85*** (−20.05)	2.18	4.02	−1.84*** (−15.93)
Downgrades	−0.81	0.70	−1.51*** (−13.34)	−4.43	−2.64	−1.79*** (−12.31)

*Note: *, ** and *** denote significance levels at 10%, 5%, and 1%, respectively.*

Table 6.
The effect of contemporaneous daily changes in VIX on the abnormal returns (ARs) around event days for the NYSE (Panel A) and the NASDAQ (Panel B).

contemporaneous VIX changes have a statistically significant effect on the abnormal returns around recommendation revisions. An increase (decrease) in VIX is associated with a smaller (larger) average AR for both upgrades and downgrades compared with the unconditional AR (see **Table 2**).

However, the results for changes in VIX are in contrast to those for changes in SKEW. Take the NYSE, day 0 and upgrades for example. For $\Delta VIX > 0$, the average AR is 0.84%, but for $\Delta VIX < 0$, it becomes larger with a value of 2.67%. These results indicate that a higher abnormal return is associated with a *decrease* in VIX (i.e., decrease in investors' fear). However, for $\Delta SKEW > 0$, the average AR is 2.25%, but for $\Delta SKEW < 0$, it becomes smaller with a value of 1.52%, which suggests that a higher abnormal return is related to an *increase* in SKEW (i.e., increase in investors' greed).

For the NASDAQ, the results are generally consistent with those for the NYSE. Again, on day −1, the corresponding magnitudes of the average AR for all cases are very close to those for the NYSE. However, on day 0, the corresponding magnitudes of the average AR are larger for the NASDAQ than for the NYSE. In the comparison between the NYSE and the NASDAQ, the results related to VIX are in line with those associated with SKEW. Overall, these results patterns could commonly be explained by the potential difference in the types of listing firms and the ways how investors perceive the firms listed on the different stock exchanges.

3.2.2 The effect on the cumulative days (−1,0)

We also examine the effect of the changes in VIX on the CARs over days −1 and 0. **Table 7** presents the results. Panel A is for the NYSE and Panel B is for the NASDAQ. Cumulative ΔVIX represents the contemporaneous cumulative changes in VIX over days −1 and 0. Our results for the NYSE are consistent with those of Kliger and Kudryavtsev [16].[12] For upgrades, the statistically significant *negative* difference indicates that the CARs are stronger when the cumulative change in VIX is *negative* (i.e., Cumulative $\Delta VIX < 0$) than that when the cumulative change in VIX is *positive* (i.e., Cumulative $\Delta VIX > 0$). However, for downgrades, the statistically significant *negative* difference suggests that the CARs are stronger when the cumulative change in VIX is *positive* (i.e., Cumulative $\Delta VIX > 0$) than that when the cumulative change in VIX is *negative* (i.e., Cumulative $\Delta VIX < 0$).

[12] Kliger and Kudryavtsev [16] do not test stocks listed on the NASDAQ.

Type of recommendation revision	CAR over days −1 and 0 (%)		
	Cumulative $\Delta VIX > 0$	Cumulative $\Delta VIX < 0$	Diff (t-statistic)
Panel A: NYSE			
Upgrades	0.73	3.28	−2.55*** (−27.70)
Downgrades	−3.32	−1.09	−2.23*** (−19.14)
Panel B: NASDAQ			
Upgrades	1.96	4.64	−2.68*** (−18.34)
Downgrades	−4.73	−2.36	−2.37*** (−12.94)

*Note: *, ** and *** denote significance levels at 10%, 5% and 1%, respectively.*

Table 7.
The effect of changes in VIX on the cumulative abnormal returns (CARs) for the NYSE (Panel A) and the NASDAQ (Panel B).

In comparison with the NYSE, we show that the corresponding magnitudes of the CARs are larger for the NASDAQ. It is in line with the argument that the telecoms industry is more sensitive to changes in investor sentiment. In short, these findings provide further evidence supporting the hypothesis stating that abnormal returns around recommendation revisions are correlated with contemporaneous changes in VIX [16].

Overall, our results of SKEW and VIX show that SKEW and VIX can act as different measures for investor sentiment in the financial markets. That is, SKEW measures investors' greed while VIX is an investors' fear gauge.

4. Conclusions

We investigate the effect of the CBOE SKEW index on the investors' reaction to analyst recommendations. We hypothesize that the abnormal returns around analyst recommendation revisions are closely correlated with contemporaneous SKEW changes. Our results for both the NYSE and the NASDAQ confirm this hypothesis. We show that when SKEW increases (i.e., increase in investors' greed) before or on the recommendation announcement days, investors could achieve higher average abnormal returns than the case with decreasing SKEW. That is, investors might gain more if they invest in stocks with upgrade recommendations during the period with an increase in SKEW. This is because investors are more optimistic and excited about the performance of the stock market. Furthermore, we observe that investors could gain higher average abnormal returns on days of upgrades and lose more on days of downgrades when investing in stocks listed on the NASDAQ than those listed on the NYSE.

We also examine the effect of VIX on the investors' reaction to analyst recommendations. The results are consistent with the findings of Kliger and Kudryavtsev [16]. Our results further demonstrate that SKEW and VIX show different effects on the financial markets. VIX is normally considered as an investors' fear gauge, but we show that SKEW could be considered as a measure for investors' greed, supported by a significantly positive relationship between the changes in SKEW and abnormal stock returns, regardless of recommendation upgrades or downgrades.

Our study complements prior literature on investor sentiment and financial markets. Han [17] documents a relation between index risk-neutral skewness [36] and investor sentiment, suggesting that the impact of investor sentiment is economically significant. With the development of various skewness measures, such as realize skewness [37], average skewness [38], systematic and idiosyncratic skewness [39], and other types of skewness [40], one of potential research directions could be examining these skewness measures in proxying investor sentiment and investors' behavior. Moreover, linking different skewness measures to a variety of corporate events (e.g., earnings announcements, dividend announcements, mergers, and acquisitions) and different stock exchanges is also worthwhile since difference skewness measures may incorporate different information, which provides useful insights for investors in making investment decisions.

JEL classification

D81; D84; G11, G14, G40.

Author details

Qingxia (Jenny) Wang[1,2]

1 Centre for Applied Climate Sciences, University of Southern Queensland, Toowoomba, Queensland, Australia

2 The University of Queensland, Brisbane, Queensland, Australia

*Address all correspondence to: jenny.wang2@usq.edu.au

References

[1] Whaley RE. Understanding the VIX. Journal of Portfolio Management. 2009; **35**(3):98-105

[2] Whaley RE. The investor fear gauge. Journal of Portfolio Management. 2000; **26**(3):12-17

[3] Smales LA. The importance of fear: Investor sentiment and stock market returns. Applied Economics. 2017; **49**(34):3395-3421

[4] Smales LA. News sentiment and the investor fear gauge. Finance Research Letters. 2014;**11**(2):122-130

[5] Fernandes M, Medeiros MC, Scharth M. Modeling and predicting the CBOE market volatility index. Journal of Banking & Finance. 2014;**40**:1-10

[6] Giot P. Relationships between implied volatility indexes and stock index returns. Journal of Portfolio Management. 2005; **31**(3):92-100

[7] Elyasiani E, Gambarelli L, Muzzioli S. Fear or Greed? What Does a Skewness Index Measure? DEMB Working Paper. 2016

[8] Mora-Valencia A, Rodríguez-Raga S, Vanegas E. Skew index: Descriptive analysis, predictive power, and short-term forecast. North American Journal of Economics and Finance. 2021;**56**: 101356

[9] Liu ZF, Faff R. Hitting skew for six. Economic Modelling. 2017;**64**: 449-464

[10] Stickel SE. The anatomy of the performance of buy and sell recommendations. Financial Analysts Journal. 1995;**51**(5):25-39

[11] Womack KL. Do brokerage analysts' recommendations have investment value? Journal of Finance. 1996;**51**(1): 137-167

[12] Barber B, Lehavy R, McNichols M, Trueman B. Can investors profit from the prophets? Security analyst recommendations and stock returns. Journal of Finance. 2001;**56**(2):531-563

[13] Jegadeesh N, Kim W. Value of analyst recommendations: International evidence. Journal of Financial Markets. 2006;**9**(3):274-309

[14] Jegadeesh N, Kim W. Do analysts herd? An analysis of recommendations and market reactions. Review of Financial Studies. 2010;**23**(2):901-937

[15] Loh RK, Stulz RM. Is sell-side research more valuable in bad times? Journal of Finance. 2018;**73**(3):959-1013

[16] Kliger D, Kudryavtsev A. Volatility expectations and the reaction to analyst recommendations. Journal of Economic Psychology. 2013;**37**:1-6

[17] Han B. Investor sentiment and option prices. Review of Financial Studies. 2008;**21**(1):387-414

[18] Sharpe SA. Reexamining stock valuation and inflation: The implications of analysts' earnings forecasts. Review of Economics and Statistics. 2002;**84**(4): 632-648

[19] Brown GW, Cliff MT. Investor sentiment and the near-term stock market. Journal of Empirical Finance. 2004;**11**(1):1-27

[20] Brown GW, Cliff MT. Investor sentiment and asset valuation. Journal of Business. 2005;**78**(2):405-440

[21] Green TC, Hwang B-H. Initial public offerings as lotteries: Skewness preference and first-day returns. Management Science. 2012;**58**(2):432-444

[22] Christie WG, Huang RD. Market structures and liquidity: A transactions data study of exchange listings. Journal of Financial Intermediation. 1994;**3**(3): 300-326

[23] Chung KH, Van Ness BF, Van Ness RA. Trading costs and quote clustering on the NYSE and NASDAQ after decimalization. Journal of Financial Research. 2004;**27**(3):309-328

[24] Weston JP. Competition on the Nasdaq and the impact of recent market reforms. Journal of Finance. 2000;**55**(6): 2565-2598

[25] Elliott WB, Warr RS. Price pressure on the NYSE and NASDAQ: Evidence from S&P 500 index changes. Financial Management. 2003:85-99

[26] Brooks RM, Patel A, Su T. How the equity market responds to unanticipated events. Journal of Business. 2003;**76**(1): 109-133

[27] Greene JT, Watts SG. Price discovery on the NYSE and the NASDAQ: The case of overnight and daytime news releases. Financial Management. 1996:19-42

[28] Kumar A. Who gambles in the stock market? Journal of Finance. 2009;**64**(4): 1889-1933

[29] Howe JS, Unlu E, Yan XS. The predictive content of aggregate analyst recommendations. Journal of Accounting Research. 2009;**47**(3):799-821

[30] Loh RK, Stulz RM. When are analyst recommendation changes influential? Review of Financial Studies. 2011;**24**(2): 593-627

[31] Jegadeesh N, Kim J, Krische S, Lee C. Analyzing the analysts: When do recommendations add value? Journal of Finance. 2004;**59**(3):1083-1124

[32] Barber B, Lehavy R, Trueman B. Comparing the stock recommendation performance of investment banks and independent research firms. Journal of Financial Economics. 2007;**85**(2):490-517

[33] Lin T-C, Lu X. Why do options prices predict stock returns? Evidence from analyst tipping. Journal of Banking and Finance. 2015;**52**:17-28

[34] Pástor Ľ, Veronesi P. Was there a Nasdaq bubble in the late 1990s? Journal of Financial Economics. 2006;**81**(1): 61-100

[35] Savor PG. Stock returns after major price shocks: The impact of information. Journal of Financial Economics. 2012; **106**(3):635-659

[36] Bakshi G, Kapadia N, Madan D. Stock return characteristics, skew laws, and the differential pricing of individual equity options. Review of Financial Studies. 2003;**16**(1):101-143

[37] Amaya D, Christoffersen P, Jacobs K, Vasquez A. Does realized skewness predict the cross-section of equity returns? Journal of Financial Economics. 2015;**118**(1):135-167

[38] Jondeau E, Zhang Q, Zhu X. Average skewness matters. Journal of Financial Economics. 2019;**134**(1):29-47

[39] Langlois H. Measuring skewness premia. Journal of Financial Economics. 2020;**135**(2):399-424

[40] Habib A, Hasan M, Jiang HY. Stock price crash risk: Review of the empirical literature. Accounting and Finance. 2018;**58**:211-251

Chapter 3

Currency and Banking Crises: The Origins and How to Identify Them

Heru Rahadyan

Abstract

Currency and banking crises have occurred periodically. Along with the growing integration and liberalisation of financial markets, there is an increasing number of currency and banking crises. This chapter shows that crises can occur in any good or bad economic conditions as they can be triggered by rational actions, panics or contagion effects. As the crises stem from various aspects, thus, they should be mitigated with different policies. Furthermore, this chapter discusses the exchange market pressure index to identify a currency crisis, the money market pressure index to identify a banking crisis and the financial market pressure index to identify the overall financial crises. Once the crises are identified, economists can start to investigate the determinants of the crises. While the probit/logit models are arguably the most popular approaches to investigating the determinants of crises, they fail to provide useful forecasts. On the other hand, while the signalling approach is considered the most successful method to forecast crises, the results are difficult to be interpreted. The empirical studies suggest that the currency and banking crises are typically preceded by a real appreciation and a lending boom, the signs of a boom period in the business cycle.

Keywords: currency and banking crises, financial crises, market pressure index, twin crisis, financial markets, financial institutions

1. Introduction

Financial crises – in particular currency crises and banking crises – have occurred periodically. The IMF reported there were 158 currency crises and 54 banking crises during 1980–1995 [1]. The collapse of the Medici Bank in the 15th century is an example of a banking failure in the early days of the development of banking. The stories of bank failure continue for centuries. The latest series of financial crises started with the subprime mortgage crisis in the US in 2007–2008 which was then followed by the banking crisis in the UK in 2008–2009 and the Spanish banking crisis.

Along with the growing integration of financial markets, financial institutions such as banks have become increasingly vulnerable to financial turmoil elsewhere. Moreover, a financial turmoil that originates from a currency crisis often develops into a banking crisis, or vice versa, giving rise to what is known as a 'twin crisis'.

This chapter explains the origins of currency and banking crises and explores different approaches to identifying the crises, as well as their determinants.

The structure of the chapter is as follows. The next section explains the origins of currency and banking crises and how to mitigate them. The third and fourth section explores different approaches to identifying the crises and their determinants, respectively. The final section concludes the chapter.

2. The origins of currency and banking crises

The models to explain the origin of currency and banking crises can be divided into three groups. The first group discusses the rational expectations of investors as the source of crises. According to this model, investors always observe the risk in their investments and act rationally. Thus, a bad macroeconomy fundamental or ineffective policy actions may trigger currency attacks or bank runs [2, 3].

The second group shows that a crisis can still occur at a good time. In this model, a crisis can be triggered by a random panic that influences investors' behaviour to massively convert their assets, thus, the crisis is self-fulfilling [4, 5].

The last group explains that a crisis can also arise in the non-existence of panic at a good time. Following this model, a crisis in other places can spread through the financial market and creates a twin currency and banking crisis [6, 7].

Interestingly, the development of the currency crisis models has gone in the opposite direction to the banking crises development. The first generation model of the crises suggests that a currency crisis stem from rational actions of investor (the speculative attack model) and a banking crisis stem from a panic attack (the random withdrawal model). On the other hand, the second-generation models of the crises argue that a currency crisis is originated from a panic attack (the self-fulfilling prophecy model) and a banking crisis is originated from a ration action (the information-based bank runs).

2.1 The rational acts as the source of currency and banking crises

The rational acts as the source of currency and banking crises can be divided into two groups. In the currency crises model, the speculative attack model argues that investors always doubt the government's ability to manage a fixed exchange rate when there is a current account deficit. When the foreign reserve is drying up to keep the exchange rate fixed, investors will attack the currency, leading to the breakdown of the fixed exchange rate regime. On the other hand, in the banking crises model, the information-based model shows that negative results in investors' risk assessment of bank portfolios may influence a bank run and create a banking crisis.

2.1.1 Speculative attack on the currency

The speculative attack model shows that investors undertake an attack if they doubt the government's capacity to keep the exchange rate fixed. Specifically, this condition occurs when the continuation of the current account deficit leads to a decline in foreign exchange reserves. As a result, the speculative attack causes the remaining reserves to move to investors, thus negatively affecting the currency [2, 8, 9].

The main contribution of the model is the idea that the speculative attack on the currency stems from a rational act rather than from investors' panic. This model succeeded in explaining the currency crisis in Latin America just a few years after it was developed, prompting researchers to examine currency crises as rational events.

The model can be explained as follow. Let us recall the domestic money market equilibrium:

$$m – p = -\alpha(i), \alpha > 0 \tag{1}$$

Where m is the money supply, p is the price level, and i is the interest rate.

The money supply is calculated based on credit (d) and foreign reserves (r), therefore:

$$m = d + r \tag{2}$$

Assuming purchasing power parity holds, we can restate the price level (p) as a fraction of the foreign price level (p^*) and the exchange rate (s), as follows:

$$p = p^* + s \tag{3}$$

Imposing uncovered interest rate parity, we can substitute the interest rate (i) with the foreign currency interest rate (i^*) and the change in the exchange rate (Δs), as follows:

$$i = i^* + \Delta s \tag{4}$$

In a fixed exchange rate regime, where s is equal to the future exchange rate (s^e), it implies that $\Delta s = 0$ and $i = i^*$. By substituting Eqs. (2)–(4) into Eq. (1) with $\Delta s = 0$, it follows that:

$$r + d – p^* - s^e = -\alpha(i^*) \tag{5}$$

Therefore, in a fixed exchange rate regime (assuming foreign currency interest rate and foreign price level are fixed), the credit grows at the same rate as the fall of the foreign reserve ($\Delta d = -\Delta r$). In the end, the foreign reserve will run out and force central banks to break the fixed exchange rate regime. Thus, the change in exchange rate policy will lead to speculative attacks which in turn lead to a crisis.

2.1.2 Information-based bank run

The information-based bank run model argues that the bank run is a logical consequence of a rational change of risk in bank portfolios [3].

In the model, there are three periods (T = 0, 1, 2) where agents have one short-term investment from T = 0 to T = 1 and one long-term investment from T = 0 to T = 2. All agents are identical at T = 0. The model imposes three assumptions: first, agents will adjust their preferences based on information on T = 1. Second, the returns on long-term investments are random. Third, long-term investment yields a zero payoff if liquidated at T = 1. Since there is no information about the returns of long-term investments, agents always observe their investments based on newly available information. If agents believe that the bank portfolio is at risk based on the latest available information, agents will withdraw their deposit. Consequently, the bank runs are information-based.

Information-based models view banks as providers of a valuable service (by creating non-marketable bank loans) rather than providers of liquidity insurance. However, non-marketable loans in the bank portfolio are difficult to monitor, thus creating asymmetric information between banks and agents.

Furthermore, agents with no interim information cannot observe the real value of a bank, thus they learn about a bank's condition by observing other depositors. However, agents cannot distinguish whether the source of withdrawal is for consumption needs or a run by informed depositors. Therefore, risk-averse agents could assume the worst-case scenario which leads to panic [10]. In addition, a noisy signal and asymmetric information between agents could lead to bank run even when the fundamentals are good enough [11].

A bank run could be efficient since there is risk-sharing between agents. However, the liquidation cost would make a bank run becomes inefficient, so central banks should intervene to control the liquidation cost [12].

Furthermore, as banks are aware that some agents receive interim information and understand the implications of different types of contracts, thus a little change in the contract will discourage agents to conduct a bank run. However, different types of a contract will have different utilities, and banks, on purpose, sometimes would choose a contract that allows a bank run [13]. Furthermore, as the information-based bank runs stem from an asymmetric information, encouraging banks to regularly publish their financial report and a statement from a credible bank supervisor may reduce the risk of bank runs.

2.2 Panics as the source of currency and banking crises

Panics as the source of currency and banking crises can be divided into two groups. In the currency crises model, the self-fulfilling prophecy model argues that the herd behaviour of investors may cause panic and lead to the withdrawal of assets. As a result, the exchange rate tends to depreciate and translates into a crisis. On the other hand, in the banking crises model, the random withdrawal model shows that depositors can do a bank run due to random events because of the lack of information held by the depositors. When there is a massive bank run, most banks will suffer from liquidity problems since banks heavily invest in long-term illiquid assets which are costly to liquidate.

2.2.1 Self-fulfilling prophecy on the exchange market

The self-fulfilling prophecy model shows that herd behaviour of investors may cause panic and lead to the withdrawal of assets. As a result, the exchange rate tends to depreciate and translates into a crisis [4].

In this model, investors' actions rely on the sequential observation of other investors' actions. If an investor observes that many other investors sell the currency, then the investor will join the herd despite his own information. Thus, the equilibrium will move from no-attack to attack equilibrium [14].

Furthermore, a lack of information between investors can also lead to an attack and breakdown of the fixed exchange rate even though there is no coordinated action between investors [15]. In this example, investors always observe the state of the economy and consider other investors' beliefs on the sustainability of a fixed exchange rate. Assuming other investors believe that the fixed exchange rate is unsustainable, investors will launch an attack if the cost of the attack is not too costly.

On the other hand, globalisation creates many investors who have identical decisions in selecting their portfolios. Driven by relative performance to other investors' performances, investors select the same portfolio with other investors to match their performances and create herding behaviour which leads to attack equilibrium [16].

The model can be explained by imposing a conditional shift in domestic credit growth into the speculative attack model [9], where the growth is G_0 if there is no attack, while credit grows faster at G_1 if there is an attack.

Figure 1 simulates the attack on conditional policy shift. $S_0{}^*$ and $S_1{}^*$ represent "shadow exchange rate lines" correlating to the rate of credit growth at G_0 and G_1 respectively. S_f is a fixed exchange rate that intersects with shadow exchange rate line $S_0{}^*$ at point A and shadow exchange rate line $S_1{}^*$ at point C.

Assuming "domestic credit" (G) is at the left side of point G^B ($G \leq G^B$), "the shadow rate" is at point B if there is no attack and jumps to point C if there is an attack. In this simulation, the "shadow rates" (S^*) are always below (or maximum at) the fixed exchange rate ($S^* \leq S_f$), thus giving no incentives to speculators to attack the fixed exchange rate.

Multiple equilibria can occur when "domestic credit" is in the range between G^A and G^B. The fixed exchange rate could be maintained if investors believe there is no chance to overcome the government (there is no immediate benefit). On the contrary, the "exchange rate" could shift to the upper "shadow rate line" ($S_1{}^*$) if investors believe there will be an attack on the currency which leads to a breakdown of the fixed exchange rate. Consequently, all investors will sell domestic currency, leading to a collapse of the fixed exchange rate. However, there are multiple equilibria in this condition since the attack can only be succeeded if there is a large investor or coordinated action of small investors to launch an attack of sufficient size.

The drawback of the self-fulfilling model is the fact that the model implies the difficulty of predicting currency crises. It implies that policymakers have a limited

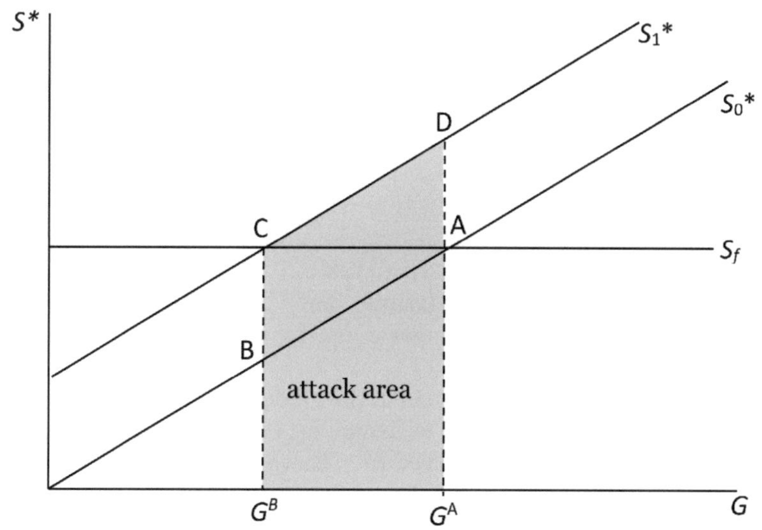

Figure 1.
Self-fulfilling prophecy with attack equilibrium.

role in managing the exchange rate since the triggers of currency crises are unclear, thus, they are difficult to forecast. However, as the attack can only succeed within a specific range of fundamentals, therefore, the policy maker can manage currency crises by managing the fundamentals [17].

2.2.2 Random withdrawal on the banking system

The random withdrawal model shows that depositors can do a bank run due to random events because of the lack of information held by the depositors. When there is a massive bank run, most banks will fail since banks heavily invest in loans that are costly to liquidate [5].

Influenced by the first-come-first-served rule, panic could occur when depositors think there will be a bank run, thus agents will try to withdraw their deposit as soon as possible before the bank collapses. Therefore, panic is self-fulfilling. Mervyn King, former Governor of the Bank of England, once said "it may not be rational to start a bank run, but it is rational to participate in one once it had started". However, panic could be avoided if banks do not follow the first-come-first-served rule. Panic will lead to expensive liquidation costs and therefore can only occur when agents are risk-averse [18].

Since the first-come-first-served rule is an essential ingredient for a bank run, eliminating this rule will also eliminate the possibility of a bank run. As an alternative to this rule, suspension of deposit convertibility in the event of a bank run [5] and variation of contracts to accommodate the possibility of a bank run (an allow-bank run contract and a run-proof contract) [18] could be considered.

Furthermore, panic could occur because the institutional structure fails to provide liquidity [19]. To avoid panic, separated-local banks will prevent agents from conducting coordinated withdrawals. Problems in separated-local banks should be addressed by a local reserve bank. Therefore, panic is related to an institutional structure in the banking system when liquidity fails to be provided. However, panic could be avoided if banks can perform an interbank loan market. Furthermore, in order to prevent panic, policymakers should force separated-local banks to hold adequate reserves [20].

In the random withdrawal model, agents use the bank as insurance against risk to cover the uncertainty of consumption needs. To do this, banks provide liquidity and guarantee when agents liquidate their investments before maturity. In doing so, banks can increase welfare but are exposed to risk. Thus, they create the possibility of a self-fulfilling bank run.

The model has three periods (T = 0, 1, 2) where agents have one short-term investment from T = 0 to T = 1 and one long-term investment from T = 0 to T = 2. All agents are identical at T = 0 and learn their type at T = 1: being a type 1 agent or being a type 2 agent who cares only about consumption in T = 1 or T = 2, respectively. The salvage value of the long-term investment is equal to the initial investment if it is interrupted at T = 1.

There are two important assumptions in the model which can lead to bank panic: agents cannot claim physical assets in exchange for their deposit, and deposit withdrawals follow the first-come-first-served rule. Based on these assumptions, there will be two equilibriums: good equilibrium occurs when type 1 agents withdraw their deposit at T = 1 and type 2 agents withdraw at T = 2, and bad equilibrium occurs when there is panic. As the liquidation of a bank's long-term assets is costly, thus, a bank will not survive if all deposits are withdrawn at once.

2.3 The contagion effects as the source of currency and banking crises

The contagion effects as the source of currency and banking crises can be divided into two groups. In the first model, the systemic risk model argues that a bank failure can create a systemic failure in the banking system through the money market. In the second model, the twin crisis model discusses how a currency crisis translates into a banking crisis or vice versa.

2.3.1 Systemic risk in banking system

The systemic risk model focuses on the propagation of a failure in one bank to other banks through financial transactions. Based on this model, interbank lending can overcome the moral hazard problem between the bank owner and depositors due to the supervision of peer banks. However, interbank lending also increases the risk of contagion for banks [6].

An interbank money market has a central role in developing systemic risk. If an interbank money market cannot support one illiquid bank, a systemic bank run may occur since agents may assume that there is not enough liquidity in the banking system. However, a problem in one bank is not sufficient to create panic. It can only be systemic when the problem occurs in a time of economic instability [21]. In addition, even though agents of one specific bank can have interim information; they do not have access to the interim information of other banks. Therefore, they will observe the number of bank failures as a proxy of interim information about macro-economic conditions and other banks' performance. In this sense, agents may conduct a bank run if they observe there are some bank failures [22].

One strand of study of systemic risk focuses on uncertainty over liquidity demand. Since agents are uncertain about where they want to consume, banks face the risk of withdrawal and the transference of agents' deposits to other areas. To address this problem, banks create an interbank money market, thus there is no need to liquidate their long-term investments to meet agents' cash demands. However, an interbank money market could make contagious bank failures when there is a gridlock in the payment system. Therefore, agents could panic when they fear there is no sufficient reserve among banks [23]. Furthermore, the interbank money market grows because of different liquidity shortages across regions. In this sense, the spread of contagion is influenced by types of claims in the interbank money market [24].

Another view of systemic risk studies the role of the unregulated banking system on systemic risk [25]. The study focuses on claims that bank failures are influenced by safety-net regulations, thus minimal regulatory intervention is required to regain financial stability. While financial market arrangement by a private institution (e.g. clearing house) is more efficient in preventing systemic shocks, a global liquidity shortage that triggers contagious runs may break down the arrangement. Therefore, an unregulated banking system is not immune to systemic risk.

2.3.2 Twin currency and banking crises

The linkages between the twin currency and banking crises are still ambiguous. It is hard to identify whether it is started by a currency or banking crisis for two reasons: First, banking and currency crises are sometimes driven by common factors [26]. Second, the currency attack and the bank run reinforced each other in a vicious circle [27].

The twin currency and banking crises model shows that the link between a currency and banking crisis lies in a problem for both foreign and domestic currency liquidity [7]. Investors start to attack the currency, either because of economic fundamentals or panic. Currency starts to depreciate and the pressure in the exchange market increases. To fund the attack, investors remove their money from banks and create pressure in the money market that can create a currency and banking crisis.

On the other hand, investors could also attack the bank, either because of random events or information-based. The cash is then used to attack the currency. To avoid sharp depreciation of the currency, the central bank starts intervening by selling foreign reserves and buying domestic currency. The money supply is contracted and pressure in the money market becomes higher. Banks start to have liquidity problems [28].

Investors will observe the central bank's capability to intervene and decide whether to continue the attack. Investors will attack the currency if the central bank indicates its defence of the currency in limited foreign reserve. However, if the central bank decides to allow the currency to depreciate, negative news and fear of depreciation may create panic and a self-fulfilling prophecy.

The central bank's intervention ceases when there is insufficient foreign reserve to sell or there is a lack of domestic currency to be bought, which then leads to a sharp depreciation of the currency. Indeed, the central bank could sterilise the intervention by buying domestic bonds. However, in many cases, the amount of available liquid and high-quality bonds is relatively limited compared to the value of an intervention (**Figure 2**).

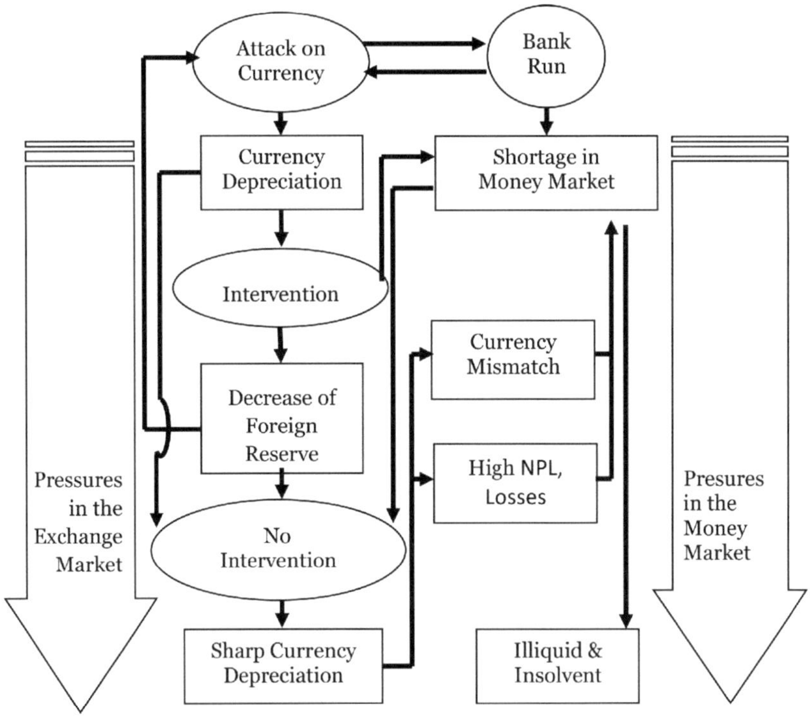

Figure 2.
Relationship between currency and banking crises.

Due to the low value of the domestic currency (and the fall of financial asset prices), demand for the domestic currency to buy foreign currency is doubled. There is a liquidity shortage in the money market which leads to a high-interest rate. Some banks will have liquidity problems and become failed banks.

Furthermore, the second-round effect of currency depreciation starts to affect banks that are exposed to foreign liabilities [29]. Some banks have currency mismatches. The third round effect affects the bank's debtors which leads to an increase in domestic and foreign currency non-performance loans (NPL). In addition, banks with foreign debt suffer from the increase in the cost of borrowing. Finally, both banks with and without foreign liabilities suffer from losses and have liquidity and insolvency problems.

The model shows that a successful intervention by the central bank may still lead to a banking crisis through the liquidity shortage channel. Furthermore, a successful attack on currency could lead to a banking crisis in two channels: on the one hand, sharp currency depreciation directly creates a currency mismatch for banks with foreign liquidity exposure. On the other hand, sharp currency depreciation affects the economy and decreases debtors' financial performance which leads to increasing NPL both for domestic and foreign currency loans. In addition, banks with foreign debt also suffer from the increasing cost of borrowing. Therefore, twin currency and banking crises should appear simultaneously.

3. The identification of currency and banking crises

The identification of currency and banking crises can be divided into three groups. In currency crises, the Exchange Market Pressure Index is arguably the most popular approach to identify the crises. In the banking crises, there is a growing interest to employ the Money Market Pressure Index to identify the crises. While the above indexes gain popularity in the currency and banking crises literature, there may be a benefit to investigating the crises as twin currency and banking crises due to interconnection in the financial market. Thus, the Financial Market Pressure model arguably provides better insight into the overall pressure on the financial market.

However, economists should employ the market pressure-based approach with caution due to the absence of consensus on how to weigh the variables and how to define the thresholds. As different weights and thresholds may lead to different crisis databases, economists may be tempted to adjust the models to fit their preferences.

3.1 Identification of currency crises

In general, there are two methods to identify currency crises. Early studies of currency crises generally use the depreciation of the exchange rate at a certain level as a basis to identify the crisis. There is no consensus about the threshold of currency depreciation to identify currency crises. For example, some economists define a currency crisis as when a currency depreciates more than 25% and there is an increase of 10% in the rate of depreciation [30].

However, using exchange rate depreciation to identify the currency crises may be biased when the central bank intervenes in order that the exchange rate does not depreciate despite considerable pressure on the currency. Even though central banks announce that they are employing an information targeting framework or a free float exchange rate regime, it is commonly acknowledged that central banks do intervene in the foreign exchange market to smooth exchange rate volatility or to maintain the exchange rate in a certain band due to the fear of floating [31].

For that reason, most recent studies use Exchange Market Pressure Index (EMPI) as the basis to identify currency crises. This model is originally developed as a monetary model to calculate the amount of foreign exchange intervention to meet a desired exchange rate target [32].

EMPI illustrates that the pressure on the exchange rate is not only reflected in the depreciation (Δe_t) but also on the amount of central bank intervention through the spot market (ΔR_t) and sometimes through the interest rate. In the event of an intervention by central banks to slow the depreciation rate, EMPI shows higher pressure in the exchange market despite there being only limited depreciation in the exchange rate.

As the variables included in the EMPI have different volatility, careful consideration of the weight associated with each variable is therefore required, so that no particular variable can distort the EMPI. Currently, there are three different popular weighting methods in the market pressure-based approaches [33–35], all of which use the standard deviation to weight the variables.

$$EMPI_t = \Delta e_t - \frac{\sigma_e}{\sigma_R} \Delta R_t \tag{6}$$

$$EMPI_t = \frac{1}{\sigma_e} \Delta e_t - \frac{1}{\sigma_R} \Delta R_t \tag{7}$$

$$EMPI_t = \frac{\frac{1}{\sigma_e}}{\left(\frac{1}{\sigma_e} + \frac{1}{\sigma_R}\right)} \Delta e_t - \frac{\frac{1}{\sigma_R}}{\left(\frac{1}{\sigma_e} + \frac{1}{\sigma_R}\right)} \Delta R_t \tag{8}$$

where σ_e is the standard deviation of the exchange rate and σ_R is the standard deviation of foreign reserve.

There is no consensus on the threshold, for example, some economists define currency crises as EMPI exceeding three standard deviations or more above the mean.

3.2 Identification of banking crises

There are two popular methods to identify banking crisis episodes. The first method is based on events, such as bank performance, government bailout, widespread bank failures, the extent of bank runs, and professional analysis to specify bank crises [36, 37].

Despite its popularity, it is difficult to identify the start date of banking crises using this event method. For example, the government's bailout normally occurs at the peak of a crisis, sometimes it involves a political process that delays the bailout.

To address the drawback of the event methods, some economists develop a Money Market Pressure Index (MMPI) as a quantitative approach to identify banking crises. The new method argues that pressure in the banking system should be reflected by the change in the interest rate. However, the central bank may conduct a monetary operation to manage the interest rate. Thus, the pressure in the banking system cannot be shown by the interest rate alone. To address this issue, the interest rate should be offset by the monetary operation [38].

MMPI can be formulated as:

$$MMPI_t = \omega_1 \Delta \gamma_t + \omega_2 \Delta i_t \tag{9}$$

Where $\Delta\gamma_t$ is changes in reserves to bank deposits ratio, Δi_t is changes in short-term real interest rate, and ω is the weight between variables.

Although the MMPI was introduced before the Global Financial Crisis of 2007–2008, it gained popularity as an approach to identifying banking crises in the aftermath of the Global Financial Crisis due to its reliability and simplicity. The index shows that while it is based on only two variables, the MMPI can identify banking crises in both developed and emerging markets [39]. In addition, the MMPI provides a clear indication of the start and end dates of banking crises - a feature that is not available in the 'so-called' event approach.

3.3 Identification of twin currency and banking crises

While there are many techniques for identifying currency and banking crises, those techniques mainly examine the crises as isolated crises. However, as the financial system is interconnected, identifying a crisis as an isolated crisis may lead to incomplete information about overall pressure in the financial system. For example, high pressures in the exchange market can be distributed to the money market, or vice versa, and create a mild pressure in both markets. Thus, the exchange market and the money market may seem stable amid high pressures on the overall financial market, which creates hidden crises [40]. Understanding these hidden crises will be the key to future mitigation policy. Therefore, there are significant benefits in considering currency and banking crises as a twin crises, rather than isolated crises.

To understand the model, let us start with the monetary equilibrium as follows:

$$M^s = M^d \tag{10}$$

where:

M^s = total money supply issued by the Central Bank.

M^d = total demand for money.

On the one hand, money is supplied by the central bank, which creates money by buying foreign reserves (F_t) and domestic assets (D_t). On the other hand, the demand for money can be represented as a function of price (P_t), income (Y_t) and interest rate (R_t). Thus, eq. (10) can be rewritten as:

$$F_t + D_t = P_t Y_t^{\beta_t} \exp\left(-\alpha_t R_t\right) \tag{11}$$

where:

β_t= income elasticity >0 at time *t*.

α_t= interest rate coefficient > 0 at time *t*.

As the money created by buying foreign reserves can be measured by multiplying foreign reserves by the exchange rate (ER_t), eq. (11) can be represented as follows:

$$(F_t.ER_t) + D_t = P_t Y_t^{\beta_t} \exp\left(-\alpha_t R_t\right) \tag{12}$$

The real measure of monetary equilibrium can be obtained by deflating the changes in the money supply by the total money supply created by the Central Bank.

$$f_t + d_t = \pi_t + \beta_t y_t - \alpha_t r_t \tag{13}$$

where:
$f_t = FR_t .ER_t / M_t$.
$d_t = \Delta D_t / M_t$.
$\pi_t = \Delta P_t / P_t$.
$y_t = \Delta Y_t / Y_t$.
$r_i (t) = \Delta R_t / d_t$.
Eq. (13) can be re-arranged to separate financial system and macroeconomic indicators as follow:

$$f_t + d_t + \alpha_t r_t = \pi_t + \beta_t y_t \quad (14)$$

In an open economy, the monetary equilibrium is affected by other countries. Thus, the interaction between country *a* and country *b* can be determined by employing the International Fisher Effect to the monetary equilibrium:

$$(f_a - f_b) + (d_a - d_b) + \alpha(r_a - r_b) = (\beta_a y_a - \beta_b y_b) + (\pi_a - \pi_b) \quad (15)$$

By adjusting the change of foreign reserves and the change of price by the rate of appreciation of currency *a* in terms of currency *b* (e_{ab}), eq. (15) can be rewritten as:

$$f_a + e_{ab} + d_a + \alpha r_a = (\beta_a y_a + \pi_a) + (f_b + d_b + \alpha r_b - \beta_b y_b - \pi_b + e_{ab}) \quad (16)$$

The $(f_a + e_{ab} + d_a + \alpha r_a)$ is referred to as the Financial Market Pressure, $(\beta_a y_a + \pi_a)$ as the Macroeconomic Pressure, and $(f_b + d_b - \beta_b y_b - \pi_b + e_{ab} + \alpha r_b)$ as the External Pressure. Thus, in the final form, eq. (16) can be represented as:

$$\textit{Financial Market Pressure} = \textit{Macroeconomic Pressure} + \textit{External Pressure}$$

The above model shows that, in a close economy, the relationship between the financial market pressure and the macroeconomic pressure should be one-on-one. However, external pressure may force the relationship to break apart.

The financial market pressure model suggests that the twin currency and banking crisis is characterised by a sharp depreciation of the exchange rate and the rise of the interest rate. To address the issues, central banks may sell their foreign reserve to stabilise the exchange rate and expand the base money. Thus, the exchange rate and the interest rate may seem stable amid high pressure in the financial system. In order to measure the total pressure in the financial market, the change in the exchange rate and the interest rate should be offset by the central bank's intervention in the exchange market and domestic money market.

4. Determinants of currency and banking crises

Following the models to identify currency and banking crises that have been described in the previous section, many empirical studies have been made to find the determinants of the currency and banking crises.

There are two popular methodologies to investigate crises. First, the multivariate probit/logit model is arguably the most popular methodology to analyse currency and banking crises [41]. This model uses the event of crisis as a dummy dependent variable with a value of one if there is a crisis and a value of zero if there is no crisis. As independent variables, a set of macroeconomic indicators is used. These binary models are occasionally also combined with the panel method when investigating a large sample of countries. One advantage of the method is that asymmetries and other non-linearities can be straightforwardly tested [42]. However, despite their popularity, binary models fail to provide useful forecasts [43].

The second strand of literature uses a non-parametric methodology to predict the currency and banking crises. One commonly used non-parametric methodology to examine currency crises is the signalling method [33]. After the crises are identified, the threshold of each variable is determined. A signal is flared when a variable exceeds a given threshold level. The variables are then investigated to calculate the correct signal, missing signal, wrong signal, or correctly do not produce a signal. Noise-to-Signal Ratio is then used to understand the ability of variables to predict systemic banking crises. As a lower Noise-to-Signal Ratio represents a low frequency of false signals, thus, the threshold level can be adjusted to find the lowest Noise-to-Signal Ratio (**Table 1**).

Noise-to-Signal Ratio can be obtained by the following formula:

$$Noise - to - SignalRatio = \frac{\frac{B}{(B+D)}}{\frac{A}{(A+C)}} \tag{17}$$

The signalling method is considered the most successful method to forecast financial crises [43]. However, the signalling method has one main drawback. It evaluates the variables individually. Thus, we need to create a composite index to measure the result. However, it is difficult to interpret the index as it is highly variable [44].

Furthermore, the most recent study employs innovative techniques such as Markov switching models [45], artificial neural networks and genetic algorithms [46], and binary recursive trees [47].

In general, the above methodologies find that the currency and banking crises are typically preceded by a real appreciation and a lending boom [35, 48]. Those two variables are signs of a boom period in the business cycle.

In a boom period, the economy typically enjoys high growth, high export and large capital inflow. High capital flow is usually dominated by hot money which is invested in portfolio instruments such as stocks and bonds. Thus, stock and bond prices start to increase [49]. On the other hand, these also lead to a real appreciation of currency [50, 51].

If real appreciation continues, exporters start to lose competitiveness which leads to decreasing export, increasing imports and a current account deficit. On the other hand, overvalued currency also provides an incentive for investors to attack the currency. Thus, the economy fundamentally becomes fragile.

Funded by capital flows, banks start pushing their lending, leading to a significant increase in speculative financing. On the other hand, to avoid the adverse effect of real appreciation, the central bank starts to intervene by buying foreign currency and

	Crisis	**No Crisis**
Signal was issued	Correct Signal (A)	False Signal (B)
No Signal was issued	Missing Signal (C)	Correctly no signal (D)

Table 1.
The classification of signals.

selling domestic currency. Both foreign reserves [52] and domestic money supply increase. Abundant liquidity encourages banks to push their lending and creates a lending boom. The bank's liquidity ratio starts to decrease, and the banking system becomes weaker.

Current account deficit pressures currency to depreciate. If foreign investors start pulling out their money, the currency depreciates faster, along with the fall of asset prices [53]. Furthermore, liquidity becomes tight, and interest rates are increasing.

Soon, firms and households will have difficulty paying the loan. Current account deficit and high non-performing loans will lead to banking crises and massive capital outflow. As a result, the currency will crash.

As fast currency depreciation is devastating, thus, the central bank tries to intervene to smooth the volatility (in the free float rate regime) or to defend the currency (in the fixed-rate regime). The success of the central bank's intervention depends on two things: the amount of foreign reserve and the amount of domestic liquidity. Even though the central bank collects sufficient foreign reserves during a boom period, the intervention may fail if there is not enough domestic currency in the market to be bought (**Figure 3**).

The above relationship also shows that there is a physical link between the currency crisis and the banking crisis, as there is a vicious cycle in economic activities. The growth may invite capital flows. However, the capital flow also stimulates growth. On the other hand, the currency attack encourages investors to withdraw their money to fund the attack. Thus, the bank run is inevitable. However, in the event of a bank run, many investors reinvest their fresh cash speculatively in foreign currency. Thus, the banking and currency crises reinforce each other in a vicious cycle. The vicious cycle suggests that the initial crisis in the twin currency and banking crisis is hard to determine.

In an empirical study, the lending boom is often represented as financial sector indicators (e.g. M2 multiplier, domestic credit/GDP, real interest rate), and real appreciation is often represented as external sector indicators (e.g. export, term of trade, real exchange rate, import, international reserve).

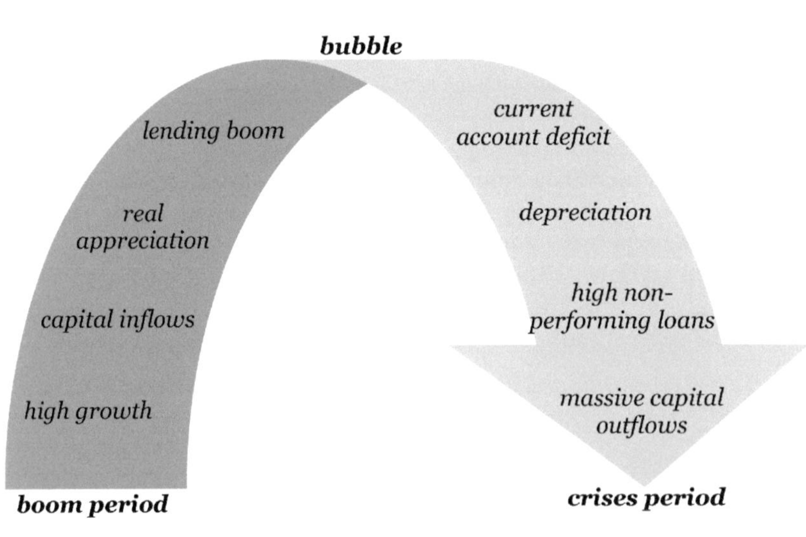

Figure 3.
The cycle of currency and banking crises.

5. Conclusions

Currency and banking crises have centuries of history, yet it is still difficult to mitigate future crises. The origins of currency and banking crises can be divided into three groups, which are rational actions, panic and contagion effect.

The first-generation model of currency crises started in the early 1980s with the speculative attack model which suggests the rational expectations of investors as the source of currency crises. In this model, investors are assumed to doubt the government's ability to manage a fixed exchange when there is a current account deficit. When the foreign reserve is drying in order to keep the exchange fixed, investors will attack the currency, leading to the breakdown of the fixed exchange rate regime.

When the speculative attack model could not explain the de facto breakdown of the European exchange rate mechanism which led to currency crises in Europe in 1992–1993, the second-generation model of currency crises which focuses on the self-fulfilling model emerged. In this model, the herd behaviour of investors may cause panic and lead to the withdrawal of assets. As a result, the exchange rate tends to depreciate and translates into a crisis. Many aspects of herd behaviour such as coordinated action of investors, sequential observation of other investors' actions and information cascade are investigated. However, herd behaviour is not the whole story since investors are unlikely to ignore their new information where potential capital gain does not depend on other investors' actions.

On the other hand, early generations of banking crises focused on random withdrawal. This model shows that depositors can do a bank run due to random events such as sunspots or economic projections due to the lack of information held by the depositors.

Unclear triggers of the bank run in the random withdrawal model encourage the emergence of the information-based model. This model shows that the bank run is a logical consequence of a rational change of risk in bank portfolios.

However, in the aftermath of the Asian financial crises of 1997–1998, new models emerge that claim currency and banking crises can still occur in the absence of panic and a well-perform economy due to contagion effects.

According to the model, failure in one bank can spread to the whole banking system through money market currency and banking crises still can occur in the absence of panic and a low-risk environment due to a contagion effect.

The systemic risk claims that interbank lending increases the systemic risk for banks. Therefore, failure in one bank can lead to the failure of many other banks. Furthermore, due to the interconnectedness of financial markets, the twin crisis model shows that a currency crisis can easily translate into a banking crisis or vice versa.

In terms of the identification of crises, early studies of currency crises generally use the depreciation of the exchange rate at a certain level as a basis for determining the crisis. However, this may be biased when the central bank intervenes so that the exchange rate does not depreciate despite considerable pressure on the currency. For that reason, most recent studies use Exchange Market Pressure Index as the basis for the determination of currency crises. This model illustrates that the pressure on the exchange rate is not only reflected in the depreciation but also in the amount of central bank intervention through the spot market (and sometimes through interest rate).

On the other hand, the definition of a banking crisis is more complicated than a currency crisis. There are various methodologies to define a banking crisis. These methodologies consider various factors such as bank performance, government bailout, widespread bank failures, extensive bank runs and professional analysis to specify bank crises. To address the complexity of the event approaches, the money market pressure index was developed to help determine the banking crisis.

In terms of methodology, while the multivariate logit model is arguably the most popular methodology for analysing currency and banking crises, it fails to provide a good forecast. On the other hand, while the signalling method is considered the most successful method to forecast financial crises, it is difficult to interpret the result as it is highly variable. The most recent study employs innovative techniques such as Markov switching models, artificial neural networks and genetic algorithms, and binary recursive trees. However, while they are much more complicated, the projection powers are still not significantly improve.

Furthermore, the empirical studies suggest that the currency and banking crises are typically preceded by a real appreciation, which is often represented as financial sector indicators (e.g. M2 multiplier, domestic credit/GDP, real interest rate) and a lending boom, which is often represented as external sector indicators (e.g. export, term of trade, real exchange rate, import, international reserve).

Acknowledgements

Thank you to Professor Catarina Figueira for her useful comments and guidance on this work.

Author details

Heru Rahadyan
Bank Indonesia, Jakarta, Indonesia

*Address all correspondence to: heru_rahadyan@bi.go.id

References

[1] Kaufman GG. Banking and currency crises and systemic risk: A taxonomy and review. Financial Markets, Institutions & Instruments. 2000;**9**(2):69-131

[2] Krugman P. A model of balance of payment crises. Journal of Money, Credit and Banking. 1979;**11**:311-325

[3] Jacklin CJ, Bhattacharya S. Distinguishing panics and information-based bank runs: Welfare and policy implications. Journal of Political Economy. 1988;**96**:568-592

[4] Obstfeld M. Rational and self-fulfilling balance-of-payments crises. The American Economic Review. 1986; **76**:72-81

[5] Diamond DW, Dybvig PH. Bank runs, deposit insurance and liquidity. Journal of Political Economy. 1983;**91**: 401-419

[6] Rochet J, Tirole J. Interbank lending and systemic risk. Journal of Money, Credit and Banking. 1996;**28**:733-762

[7] Rahadyan H, Figueira C. The dynamics of twin -banking and currency crises: The role of market pressure. In: The 24th Annual Global Conference. Hempstead, New York: Global Finance Association; 2017a

[8] Salant S, Henderson D. Market anticipation of government policies and the price of gold. Journal of Political Economy. 1978;**86**:627-648

[9] Flood R, Marion N. Perspectives on the recent currency crisis literature. International Journal of Finance and Economics. 1999;**4**:1-26

[10] Chari V, Jagannathan R. Banking panics, information, and rational expectations equilibrium. The Journal of Finance. 1988;**XLIII**(3):750-761

[11] Goldstein I, Pauzner A. Demand-deposit contracts and the probability of bank runs. The. Journal of Finance. 2005; **LX(3)**:1293-1327

[12] Allen F, Gale D. Optimal financial crises. The Journal of Finance. 1998;**LIII** (4):1245-1284

[13] Alonso I. On avoiding bank runs. Journal of Monetary Economics. 1996;**37**: 73-87

[14] Banerjee A. A simple model of herd behavior. Quarterly Journal of Economics. 1992;**107**:797-817

[15] Morris S, Shin HS. Informational events that trigger currency attack. Federal Reserve Bank of Philadelphia Working Paper, No. 95-24. 1995. pp. 1-40. Available from: https://economics.mit.edu/files/20059

[16] Calvo GA, Mendoza EG. Rational herd behavior and the globalization of securities markets. Federal Reserve Bank of Minneapolis, Institute for Empirical Macroeconomics Discussion Paper, No. 120. 1997. pp. 1-30. Available from: https://www.minneapolisfed.org/research/DP/DP120.pdf

[17] Jeanne O. Currency crises: A perspective on recent theoretical developments. Centre for Economic Policy Research Discussion Paper, No. 2170. 1999. pp. 1-42. Available from: https://repec.cepr.org/repec/cpr/ceprdp/Dp2170.pdf

[18] Cooper R, Ross TW. Bank runs: Liquidity and incentives. NBER Working Paper, No. 3921. 1991. pp. 1-38. Available

from: https://www.nber.org/system/files/working_papers/w3921/w3921.pdf

[19] Wallace N. Another Attempt to Explain an Illiquid Banking System: The Diamond-Dybvig Model with Sequential Service Taken Seriously. Quarterly Review: Federal Reserve Bank of Minneapolis; 1988

[20] Chari V. Banking without deposit insurance or bank panics: Lessons from a model of the U.S. national banking system. Federal Reserve Bank of Minneapolis, Quarterly Review. 1989;**13**(2):3-19. Available from: http://minneapolisfed.org/research/qr/qr1331.pdf

[21] Bougheas S. Contagious bank runs. International Review of Economics and Finance. 1999;**8**:131-146

[22] Chen Y. Banking panics: The role of the first-come, first served rule and information externalities. Journal of Political Economy. 1999;**107**:946-968

[23] Freixas X, Parigi BM, Jean-Charles R, Krishnamurthy A. Systemic risk, interbank relations, and liquidity provision by the central bank. Journal of Money, Credit, and Banking. 2000; **32**(3):611-638

[24] Allen F, Gale D. Financial contagion. Journal of Political Economy. 2000; **108**(1):1-33

[25] Aghion P, Bolton P, Dewatripont M. Contagious bank failures in a free banking system. European Economic Review. 2000;**44**:713-718

[26] Glick R, Hutchison M. Banking and currency crises: How common are twins? Federal Reserve Bank of San Francisco, Center for Pacific Basin Monetary and Economic Studies Working Paper, No. PB99-07. 1999. pp. 1-41. Available from: https://www.frbsf.org/economic-research/wp-content/uploads/sites/4/wppb99-07.pdf

[27] Schnabel I. The german twin crises of 1931. The Journal of Economic History. 2004;**64**(3):822-871

[28] Stoker J. Intermediation and the Business Cycles under a Specie Standard: The Role of the Gold Standard in English Financial Crises, 1790–1850. Mimeo: University of Chicago; 1994

[29] Mishkin FS. Understanding financial crises: A developing country perspective. In: Annual World Bank Confrence on Developing Economics. Washington DC: World Bank; 1996. pp. 29-62

[30] Frankel JA, Rose AK. Currency crashes in emerging markets: An empirical treatment. Journal of International Economics. 1996;**41**:351-366

[31] Calvo G, Reinhart C. Fear of floating. NBER Working Paper Series, No. 7993. 2000. pp. 1-31. Available from: https://www.nber.org/system/files/working_papers/w7993/w7993.pdf

[32] Girton L, Roper D. A monetary model of exchange market pressure applied to the postwar Canadian experience. The American Economic Review. 1977;**67**(4):537-548

[33] Kaminsky G, Lizondo S, Reinhart CM. Leading indicators of currency crises. IMF Staff Papers. 1998;**45**:1-48

[34] Eichengreen B, Rose A, Wyplosz C. Exchange market mayhem: The antecedents and aftermath of speculative attacks. Economic Policy. 1995;**21**:249-312

[35] Sachs JD, Tornel A, Velasco A. Financial crises in emerging markets: The lesson from 1995. Brooking Papers on Economic Activity. 1996;**1**:147-215

[36] Demirguc-Kunt A, Detragiache E. The determinants of banking crises in developed and developing countries. IMF Staff Paper. 1998;**45**(1): 81-109

[37] Caprio G, Klingebiel D. Bank insolvencies: Cross-country experience. World Bank Policy Research Working Paper, No. 1620. 1996. pp. 1-52. Available from: https://documents1.worldbank.org/curated/en/761051468739458460/pdf/multi-page.pdf

[38] Von Hagen J, Ho T-K. Money market pressure and the determinants of banking crises. Journal of Money, Credit and Banking. 2007;**39**(5):1037-1066

[39] Jing Z, de Haan J, Jacobs J, Yang H. Identifying banking crises using money market pressure: New evidence for a large set of countries. Journal of Macroeconomics. 2015;**43**:1-20

[40] Rahadyan H, Figueira C. Financial Market Pressure Index and the Dynamics of Generalized Financial Crisis. Annual EEFS Conference 2017. Ljubljana: European Economics and Finance Society; 2017b

[41] Frankel J, Saravelos G. Can leading indicators assess country vulnerability? Evidence from the 2008-09 global financial crisis. Journal of International Economics. 2012;**87**:216-231

[42] Aron J, Macdonald R, Muellbauer J. Exchange rate pass-through in developing and emerging markets: A survey of conceptual, methodological and policy issues, and selected empirical findings. The Journal of Development Studies. 2014;**50**(1):101-143

[43] Berg A, Pattilo C. Are currency crises predictable? A test. IMF Staff Papers. 1999;**46**(2):107-138

[44] Edison HJ. Do indicators of financial crises work? An evaluation of an early warning system. International Journal of Finance and Economics. 2003;**8**:11-53

[45] Heriqbaldi U. Exchange market pressure in Indonesia: A univariate markov switching analysis. Asian Economic and Financial Review. 2012; **2**(5):603-616

[46] Apoteker T, Barthelemy S. Genetic algorithms and financial crises in emerging markets. Colloque International de Sienne. 2000:1-15. Available from: https://citeseerx.ist.psu.edu/viewdoc/download;jsessionid=41FBA97E81BDB716D0F108C30F2AA67A?doi=10.1.1.116.8451&rep=rep1&type=pdf

[47] Frankel J, Wei SJ. Managing macroeconomic crises. NBER Working Paper Series, No. 10907. 2004. pp. 1-86. Available from: https://www.nber.org/system/files/working_papers/w10907/w10907.pdf

[48] Tornell A, Westermann F. Boom-bust cycles in middle income countries: Facts and explanation. NBER Working Paper Series. 2002;**9219**:1-45

[49] Aliber RZ. The 36 most tumultuous years in monetary history: Shocks, the transfer problem, and financial trauma. IMF Staff Paper. 2005;**52**:142-159

[50] Velasco A. Financial crises and balance of payments crises. Journal of Development Economics. 1987;**27**: 263-283

[51] Weller CE. Financial crises after financial liberalisation: Exceptional circumstances or structural weakness. The Journal of Development Studies. 2001;**38**(1):98-127

[52] Aizenman J, Hutchison MM. Exchange market pressure and

absorption by international reserves: Emerging markets and fear of reserve loss during the 2008-2009 crisis. Journal of International Money and Finance. 2012;**31**:1076-1091

[53] Singh R. Asset prices and twin crises. Journal of International Money and Finance. 2009;**28**(1):26-55. Available from: https://www.sciencedirect.com/science/article/abs/pii/S0261560608001137

Chapter 4

Current Challenges to World Financial Stability: To What Extent is the Past a Guide for the Future?

Alex Cukierman

Abstract

The chapter discusses current challenges to world financial stability in light of lessons that have been learned from past financial crises. Although there are parallels between the current situation and some of the previous crises, the current situation differs in several important respects. It comes after a decade of extremely low nominal and real interest rates along with subdued inflation and, due to fiscal and monetary policy measures deployed during the GFC and the COVID-19 pandemic, debt/GDP ratios and central banks (CBs) balance sheets are at historically high levels. The recent upsurge of inflation prompted a worldwide process of increase in policy interest rates and reduction in CB assets. An undesirable side effect of this process is that it may trigger several mechanisms that endanger world financial stability. Recent developments in Fintech and the global economic disruptions caused by the war in Ukraine create novel financial vulnerabilities that differ from previous financial crises. The rapid growth of fintech institutions poses new regulatory challenges at the national and international levels. Although no crisis has materialized to date, those developments have increased the odds of a systemic global crisis. Measures designed to mitigate financial vulnerabilities are briefly discussed in the concluding section.

Keywords: past financial crises, inflation, regulatory challenges of fintech, Ukraine war and global stability, remedial devices

1. Introduction

A common thread of past financial crises is that they all occur following a period of (expost) exaggerated economic optimism characterized by rapid credit expansion against a backdrop of underdisciplined fiscal/monetary policies and lax regulatory institutions. The credit expansion is accompanied by high investments, high economic activity, and increased prices in assets and real estate markets. In the absence of sufficiently large economic or political shocks, this happy state may last for a while.

However, when an unanticipated adverse shock materializes, lenders stop lending and demand immediate repayment on short-term loans triggering default, panic, contagion, and ultimately runs also on some solvent institutions. This leads to violent reversals in asset markets and contraction in real economic activity. The mechanisms through which this process materialized in past crises differ depending on a country's institutions, level of development, depth of the capital market, structure of the banking system exchange rate arrangements, inflation differentials, central bank independence, and political stability.

The chapter discusses current challenges to world financial stability in light of the lessons that have been learned from past financial crises, such as the global financial crisis (GFC), and some of the older crises in Asia, Latin America, and Russia. Although there are parallels between the current situation and some of the buildup toward those previous crises, the current situation differs in several important respects. First, it comes after a decade of extremely low nominal and real interest rates along with subdued inflation. Second, due to fiscal and monetary policy measures deployed during the GFC and the COVID-19 pandemic, debt/GDP ratios and central banks (CBs) balance sheets are at historically high levels. The recent upsurge of inflation (due to both supply and demand factors) prompted a worldwide process of increase in policy interest rates and a gradual reduction in CB assets. Those policy trends are likely to intensify over the foreseeable future. An undesirable side effect of this process is that it may trigger several mechanisms that endanger world financial stability.

Recent developments in Fintech and the global economic disruptions caused by the war in Ukraine create novel financial vulnerabilities that differ from those of previous financial crises. The rapid growth of fintech institutions in banking and other financial intermediaries poses new regulatory challenges at the national and international levels, and none of the previous crises was triggered by war. Although no crisis has materialized as of yet (July 2022), those developments have increased the odds of a systemic global crisis.

The chapter is organized as follows: Section 2 describes the major financial crises in the post-World War II (WW-II) period. Section 3 draws lessons from those crises for the future, and Section 4 discusses the new risks created by the recent acceleration in the growth of fintech, by the reduction in world trade and rising commodity prices due to the Russian invasion of Ukraine, and the rise of Chinese overseas lending for global financial stability. This is followed by concluding remarks.

2. An overview of post-world war II financial crises

2.1 The 1980s Latin American debt crisis[1]

The 1973 and 1979 oil shocks created current account deficits in many Latin American (LA) countries. In parallel, these shocks created substantial current account surpluses in the oil-exporting countries. With the encouragement of the US government, large banks became intermediaries between the two groups, providing the oil-exporting countries with a safe dollar-denominated, liquid asset and lending those funds mostly in dollars to Latin America (FDIC).

World economic expansion and low real rates on short-term loans made this situation tenable during the seventies. But this changed when Federal Reserve (Fed) chairman Volcker and other Western CBs raised interest rates to contain the inflation of the seventies, creating a worldwide recession in the early eighties. Commercial banks

[1] This subsection draws partially on Ref. [1, 2].

raised rates and shortened repayment periods. As a result, LA countries discovered that their debt burdens were unsustainable.

The crisis erupted in August 1982, when the Mexican finance minister informed US authorities and the International Monetary Fund (IMF) that Mexico would no longer be able to service its debt. Other countries quickly followed this path. Ultimately 16 LA countries and 11 less-developed countries (LDCs) in other parts of the world rescheduled their debts. In response, many banks stopped new overseas lending and tried to collect and restructure existing debt portfolios. Funds scarcity in the debtor countries plunged them into recessions and triggered devaluations of domestic currencies and inflation.

Initially, US banking regulators allowed lenders to delay recognition of the full extent of overseas lending in their loan loss provisions. By 1989, US Secretary of the Treasury Brady proposed a plan that would permanently reduce loan principal and debt service obligations conditional on the undertaking of domestic structural reforms in debtor countries. The plan was backed and partially financed by the IMF and the US Treasury. Ultimately about one-third of the total debt of the 18 countries that signed on to the plan was forgiven.

2.2 The 1997/98 Asian financial crisis[2]

Prior to the crisis, most of the Far Eastern countries that were involved in the crisis did very well. Business-friendly policies and cautious fiscal and monetary policies had translated into high rates of savings and investment, supporting GDP growth rates exceeding 5% and often approaching 10%.

However, as the crisis unfolded, it became clear that the strong growth record of these economies had masked important vulnerabilities. Years of rapid domestic credit growth and inadequate supervisory oversight had resulted in a significant build-up of leverage and doubtful loans. Industrial policies of governments led corporations and banks to believe that, in case of financial difficulties, they will be bailed out in spite of the fact that there was no official commitment to such bailouts (see Ref. [4]).

Overheating domestic economies and real estate markets added to the risks and led to increased reliance on foreign savings. This was reflected in mounting current account deficits and a build-up in external debt. Heavy foreign borrowing, often at short maturities, also exposed corporations and banks to exchange rate and funding risks. Prior to the crisis, those risks had been masked by longstanding currency pegs. When the crisis erupted, most of those pegs proved unsustainable and firms saw sharp increases in the local currency value of their external debts, leading many into distress and even insolvency.

The crisis burst into the open on July 2 1997 when, following months of speculative pressures that had depleted its foreign exchange reserves, Thailand devalued its currency relative to the U.S. dollar. In subsequent months, Thailand's currency, equity, and property markets weakened further as its difficulties evolved into a twin balance-of-payments and banking crisis. Malaysia, the Philippines, and Indonesia also allowed their currencies to weaken in the face of market pressures, with Indonesia gradually falling into a financial and political crisis. Severe balance-of-payments pressures in South Korea brought the country to the brink of default. Hong Kong faced several large but unsuccessful speculative on its peg to the dollar, the first of which triggered short-term stock market sell-offs across the globe. Across East Asia, capital inflows

[2] This subsection draws on Ref. [3].

slowed or reversed direction, and growth slowed sharply. Banks came under significant pressure, investment rates plunged, and some Asian countries entered deep recessions, producing important spillovers to trading partners across the globe.

In response to the spreading crisis, the IMF, the World Bank, the Asian Development Bank, and governments in the Asia-Pacific region, Europe, and the U.S. provided large loans to help the crisis countries rebuild official reserves and buy time to restore confidence and stabilize their economies, while also minimizing lasting disruptions to countries' relations with their external creditors. To address the structural weaknesses exposed by the crisis, aid was conditional on substantial domestic policy reforms. These included measures to deleverage, clean up and strengthen weak financial systems and improvement of competitiveness. Countries hiked interest rates to help stabilize currencies and tightened fiscal policy to speed external adjustment and cover the cost of bank clean-ups. But, as markets began to stabilize, the macro policy mix evolved to include some loosening of fiscal and monetary policies to support growth.

2.3 The 1998 Russian financial crisis[3]

The Russian crisis took place in the first decade of Russia's 1991 transition from a centrally planned economy to a free market economy. During the first years of the transition, GDP declined sharply, poverty became widespread, and inflation reached hyperinflationary dimensions. Between 1994 and 1996, inflation was stabilized, fiscal policy was tightened, and there was a substantial reduction in GDP shrinkage. The willingness of the Russian government to enter negotiations about a payment rescheduling of the former Soviet debt in April 1996 along with some financial aid from the IMF and the World Bank Union signaled improving relations with the West and had a positive impact on investors' confidence and revived the Russian capital market. This was amplified by a recovery in the international price of oil—a major Russian export product.

However, in the fourth quarter of 1997, market sentiment deteriorated drastically as a result of the Asian financial crisis. In November 1977, the Russian ruble came under speculative attack. The CB of Russia (CBR) defended the fixed peg and lost in the process a quarter of its Foreign Exchange (Forex) reserves. The Asian crisis led to a decrease in the price of oil, delivering another blow to the Russian economy. As market sentiment deteriorated, investors became aware of Russia's domestic weaknesses. Poor tax collection, widespread tax evasion, and corruption raised the budget deficit and the balance of payments deficits. The first war in Chechnya imposed additional tax burdens.

By mid-1998, international liquidity was low and Russia's current account deteriorated further as oil prices continued to fall. In an attempt to support the ruble and reduce capital flight, the interest rate was hiked to 150% by the CBR. In July 1998, monthly interest payments on Russia's debt exceeded monthly tax collections. Parliamentary disapproval of an anti-crisis plan completely eroded investors' confidence, triggering runs on domestic banks. Many banks were closed and many depositors lost their savings. The crisis resulted in a renewed strong contraction of the economy and also affected investor confidence in emerging markets worldwide.

Thanks to the depreciation of the ruble, the banks restructuring, and the increase in international oil prices, the Russian economy recovered rather quickly.

[3] This subsection partially draws on Ref. [5].

2.4 The 1998/99 Brazilian crisis[4]

In 1994, after years of failed price stabilization and high inflation, Brazil initiated a stabilization plan named after its currency—the real. Under the Real Plan, the federal government took steps to correct a large budget deficit by reducing transfers to states and municipalities and increasing federal taxes. Monetary policy was tightened, and the real was pegged to the dollar with gradual adjustments through a crawling peg. During 1998, the plan practically eliminated inflation that had reached hyperinflationary dimensions, but balance-of-payments problems persisted.

Brazil's fundamentals on the eve of the crisis taken alone would not have necessarily deteriorated into a financial crisis. But it was affected by financial contagion from the 1997 crisis and the 1998 Russian crisis. As described above, those two crises substantially reduced international liquidity. International investors withdrew funds not only from the affected countries but also from economies with a poor past record of economic management, such as Brazil. To discourage the consequent outflow of dollars, the CB of Brazil raised interest rates sharply losing in the process half of its forex reserves. High-interest rates dramatically increased Brazil's overall budget deficit through the debt service component.[5] In addition, debt maturity was shortened, making this burden more immediate. This obviously spooked investors even more.

The IMF made a commitment to provide funds designed to soften forex hemorrhage, and the Brazilian government was supposed to pass legislation designed to reduce the budget deficit. When this legislation was rejected by Congress and the governor of Minas Gerais announced that he would suspend his state's debt payments to Brazil's national government for 3 months' attacks against the currency intensified.

By mid-January 1999, Brazil announced that pegging was over and its exchange rate would be allowed to float.

2.5 The Argentine 2001/2 crisis[6]

Due to political and monetary instability, Argentina had a record of extremely high and persistent inflation in the post-WW II period. Numerous efforts at inflation stabilization quickly failed due to undisciplined fiscal institutions and political interference at the CB. When inflation reached over 3000% per year, plans for economic stabilization and liberalization were deployed in 1989. The reforms included the privatization of state-owned enterprises, the deregulation of the economy, lower trade barriers state reform, and, last but not least, the Convertibility Plan of 1991, which fixed the Argentine peso one-to-one to the US Dollar. Under this currency board, Argentines could now freely convert their pesos into dollars. From then on, bank deposits and loans in dollars became widespread. Moderately expansive fiscal policy stimulated the economy and helped restore economic growth.

With the implementation of the reforms, Argentina won great commendation, especially from the IMF. On Wall Street, Argentina became one of the most favorite emerging markets and became the biggest issuer of emerging markets debt in the late nineties. This made the country increasingly dependent on foreign capital. Following the implementation of reforms, the Argentine economy entered a period of economic growth between 1991 and 1997. Only in 1995 output growth was negative, due to the

[4] This subsection draws on FRB of Dallas [6].

[5] The primary deficit was much smaller.

[6] This subsection partially draws on Ref. [7].

so-called Tequila crisis in Mexico. But the quick return of high economic growth in 1996 suggested that the Argentine economy was strong enough to counter external shocks. This further strengthened the confidence in the implemented policies, including the Convertibility Plan.

The outbreak of currency crises in Asia, Russia, and Brazil in 1997/1998 increased the borrowing costs for emerging markets, including Argentina. Furthermore, in 1998 when Brazil, a major trading partner of Argentina, ended its own peg to the US dollar, Argentina became less competitive. In addition, the prices of Argentina's agricultural export products fell and the US dollar appreciated reaching its highest level in 15 years. All this led to a sharp reduction in exports. As a result, Argentina's current account deficit rose and the country went into recession in the autumn of 1998.

Initially, Argentina maintained its peg, but this left it unable to respond to the growing economic imbalances. The fact that the exchange rate peg was not supported by nominal price and wage flexibility further reduced Argentina's means to deal with the currency overvaluation and decreased the credibility of the fixed exchange rate regime. As a consequence, foreign investors lost confidence in the Argentine economy, the country experienced a strong increase in borrowing costs and, by July 2001, the country had fully lost its access to international financial markets. This untenable problem was aggravated further by a procyclical fiscal policy.

At the end of December 2001, in a climate of severe political and social unrest, Argentina partially defaulted on its USD 93 billion international debt and 2 months later formally abandoned the Convertibility Plan. The pesofication of bank deposits and loans at two different exchange rates and prize freezes for utility companies caused a wave of defaults and liquidity problems at Argentine companies as well as at domestic and foreign banks. Among others, Argentina's largest locally owned private-sector bank, Banco Galicia, and several foreign banks, such as Bank of America, Citigroup, FleetBoston, and J.P. Morgan Chase & Co, suffered heavy losses.

2.6 The 2007/2014 global financial crisis (GFC)

Unlike all the crises described above, the GFC erupted in the US—the epicenter of world financial markets—sending shock waves throughout global financial markets. The crisis was preceded by 20 years of subdued economic fluctuations known as "the great moderation." Between 2004 and 2007, a real estate boom swept the US and other Western economies. During that period, the volume of mortgage-backed securities (MBS) increased by leaps and bounds. MBS are bonds secured by large packages of mortgages that are divided into default risk tranches with higher risk tranches carrying higher rates. This repackaging of mortgages supplied to saving institutions a safe asset at slightly higher rates than other bonds of similar risk and dramatically increased the supply of funds to mortgage banks. Pension funds, insurance companies, and hedge funds all over the world absorbed large quantities of MBS.

The persistently rising real estate properties prior to the crisis led mortgage banks to finance most, and at time all or more, of the acquisition cost of a house. Under those circumstances, mortgage borrowers effectively borrowed with very little or no equity at all. This happy state lasted as long as real estate prices continued to rise. But, when they stopped rising and started to decline in 2006/7, the atmosphere changed. Many mortgage borrowers who had bought second and third homes stopped servicing their debt and returned the keys to their house to banks. In turn, the banks put those houses on the market at dumping prices, strengthening the decrease in prices.

As this happened, the riskiness of MBS increased, and their prices decreased triggering calls for further funds from affected thrift institutions.[7]

This process was particularly devastating for highly leveraged hedge funds. Hedge funds owned by major investment banks defaulted pushing their parent companies into default. The most prominent downfalls among those were Bear-Stern in March 2008 and Lehman Brothers in September 2008. Shortly after, it became evident that the American International Group (AIG), a worldwide insurance company, and Fannie Mae and Freddie Mac, which together account for about half of the U.S. mortgage market, were on the verge of collapse endangering the entire US financial system.

On October 3 2008, following desperate and well-documented pleas for fiscal bailouts by Fed Chair Bernanke and Secretary of the Treasury Paulson, Congress created a $700 billion Troubled Asset Relief Program (TARP) to bailout failing institutions by buying MBS and other securities whose value had decreased dramatically and which became known as "toxic assets."[8] In parallel, the Fed reduced the federal funds rate (FFR) to zero and engaged in large scale asset purchases (LSAP) also known as quantitative easing (QE). Since the FFR had been reduced to the zero lower bound (ZLB), QE became the main instrument of monetary policy and was used extensively during the six or so years of the GFC. Congress also approved a separate package to bailout Fannie Mae and Freddie Mac. Within several months, those extraordinary rescue operations stabilized the financial panic that engulfed markets following Lehman's collapse, and within a couple of years, Fannie Mae, Freddie Mac, and AIG repaid all their debts to the federal government. However, unemployment remained above 5% until the end of 2014 ([8], Figure 1). New bond issues and banking credit were also depressed till at least the end of 2014 and, except for an upward blip in 2011, inflation was well below 2%.

In parallel, the Eurozone (EZ) had its own crisis. Summary information on the evolution of the GFC in Europe appears in Ref. [9]. Following the near meltdown of their financial systems, regulators in the U.S. and the EZ recognized the damages that can be inflicted on the economy via the failure of a "too big to fail" institution and the importance of systemic supervision and regulation. This led to a series of regulatory reforms on both sides of the Atlantic, the most important of which is the creation of systemic regulators and the exante identification of systemically important institutions (SIFI). Further details appear in Ref. [10].

3. The legacy of past crises and current challenges

3.1 Lessons from Volcker's disinflation for the present

During the GFC, the balance sheets (BSs) of Western CB expanded at rates never seen before. In particular, between 2008 and 2014, the BS of the Fed increased by a factor of 4.5. In 2016, the Fed made a modest effort at tapering but, as soon as the COVID-19 pandemic hit the globe at the beginning of 2020, substantial QE operations were resumed in order to help the Treasury finance huge aid packages to

---

[7] From a peak of over one trillion and a half in 2006, net new issues of MBS plus municipal bonds became negative in 2008, remained in negative or negligible territory every single year until 2013, and rose very modestly above zero through 2017 ([8], Section 2.3 and Figure 4).

[8] An illuminating discussion of the tortuous process that led to the adoption of the TARP legislation appears in Ref. [11].

individuals and corporations in the economy. As a consequence, between the end of 2019 and the end of 2021, the BS of the Fed doubled. This policy paid off for the US as it stimulated the economy and reduced unemployment in spite of the obstacles posed by the pandemic.[9] However frequent lockouts in China and elsewhere along with the war in Ukraine revived inflation prompting CBs in many countries to increase policy rates. Initially, the Fed did not move the FFR away from the vicinity of the ZLB. But as U.S. inflation accelerated to around 8%, it finally engaged in a gradual process of rates lifting in March 2022.

The current situation is reminiscent of Volcker's disinflation at the beginning of the eighties. In both cases, an important portion of the inflation is due to aggregate supply factors; a dramatic increase in the price of oil by OPEC then and, currently, an increase in this price due to sanctions on Russia in response to the invasion of Ukraine. As Ukraine and Russia are major suppliers of cereals and wheat, the war also reduces world supplies of those staples causing a general increase in food prices. In both cases, CBs respond to rising inflation by raising policy rates. As recounted in Section 2.1, Volcker's disinflation was one of the factors contributing to the LA crisis in the early 1980s.

But there also are differences between those two episodes. Most importantly, due to fiscal and monetary policy measures deployed during the GFC and the COVID-19 pandemic, debt/GDP ratios, private debts, and CBs balance sheets of the U.S. and other Western economies are at historically high levels. By contrast, the levels of public and private debt in the early eighties were much lower. In addition, the current round of rate lifting comes after a decade of extremely low nominal and real interest rates along with subdued inflation. By raising the debt service of private and public borrowers and depressing the value of assets, overly quick lifting of rates, may create strains on business and public finances pushing marginal borrowers to the brink of default. The experience of the LA crisis in the 1980s suggests that this risk is relatively more important for emerging markets with limited access to international capital markets than for developed economies. For advanced economies, such risks are mitigated by the comprehensive regulatory reforms that have been implemented during the GFC.

3.2 The sovereign-Bank nexus[10]

The pandemic has left emerging-market banks holding record levels of government debt, increasing the odds that pressures on public-sector finances could threaten financial stability. According to Chapter 2 of the IMF's April 2022 Global Financial Stability Report [12], the average ratio of public debt to gross domestic product rose to a record 67% last year in emerging market countries. Emerging-market banks have provided most of that credit, driving holdings of government debt as a percentage of their assets to a record 17% in 2021. In some economies, government debt amounts to a quarter of bank assets. As a result, emerging-market governments rely heavily on their banks for credit, and these banks rely heavily on government bonds as an investment that they can use as collateral for securing funding from the central bank.

This interdependence carries the seeds of financial instability. Large holdings of sovereign debt expose banks to losses if government finances come under pressure and the market value of government debt declines. That could force

[9] By contrast economic activity in some EZ countries is still low.

[10] This subsection draws on chapter 1 of the April 2022 Global Financial Stability Report [12] and on Ref. [13].

banks—especially those with less capital—to curtail lending to companies and households, weighing on economic activity. As the economy slows and tax revenues shrink, government finances may come under even more pressure, further squeezing banks. The sovereign-bank nexus could lead to a self-reinforcing adverse feedback loop that ultimately could force the government into default triggering a, so-called, "doom loop" between domestic banks and government debt. Such a loop reinforced the 1998 Russian crisis and the 2001–2002 Argentinian crisis.

Emerging-market (EM) economies are at greater risk to experience this "doom loop" than advanced economies for two reasons. First, their growth prospects are weaker relative to the pre-pandemic trend compared with advanced economies, and governments have less fiscal firepower to support the economy. Second, external financing costs of EM have generally risen, so governments have to pay more to borrow. The recent sharp tightening of global financial conditions—resulting in higher interest rates and weaker currencies on the back of monetary policy normalization in advanced economies and intensifying geopolitical tensions caused by the war in Ukraine—could undermine investor confidence in the ability of EM governments to repay debts. A domestic shock, such as an unexpected economic slowdown, could have the same effect.

3.3 Strains on public finances in emerging markets

More generally, strains on public finance in EM with limited access to credit constitute another vulnerability. For example, Government programs, such as deposit insurance, intended to support banks in times of stress may trigger systemic financial fears. Strains on government finances could hurt the credibility of those guarantees, weaken investor confidence, and ultimately hurt banks' profitability. Troubled lenders would then have to turn to government bailouts, further straining public-sector finances.

Another risk channel works through the broader economy. A blow to public finances could push economy-wide interest rates higher, hurting corporate profitability and increasing credit risk for banks. That in turn would limit banks' ability to lend to households and other corporate customers, curbing economic growth and making the economy more vulnerable to unexpected shocks. Further details appear in chapter 2 of the April 2022 Global Financial Stability Report.

3.4 Risks to financial stability in the presence of substantial public and private forex debt

In many emerging markets, such as LA countries and Eastern European economies, a non-negligible part of both the public and the private debt is denominated in forex. In the past, the debt was usually owed to financial centers in developed economies. This phenomenon is known as "the original sin." In some of the financial crises described in Section 2, persistent inflation differentials between such an EM and the economies of the lenders, or any other adverse shock to the domestic economy, may trigger downward pressures on the local currency. This risk is mitigated by persistent balance-of-payments surpluses and adequate forex reserves. However, previous experience suggests that in the absence of such cushions, an EM is likely to experience capital outflows, increases in the cost of debt, shortening of maturities, and downward pressures on the exchange rate. On the other, a new data set suggests that in many EMs, this risk is currently substantially lower than in the past for several reasons. External financing has shifted from forex debt to foreign direct investments

(FDI), portfolio equity investments, and local currency debt, and most EMs possess now larger amounts of forex currency assets (details appear in Ref. [14]).

4. Financial stability implications of Fintech, the war in Ukraine, and the rise of Chinese overseas lending

The financial stability risks posed by Fintech and the war in Ukraine are relatively novel. The current level of digitization and technological innovations in financial activities—Fintech in short—is a relatively new phenomenon and the Russian invasion of Ukraine was a largely unanticipated event at the beginning of 2022. Chinese overseas lending expanded vigorously during the last decade, and as of 2017, it became the largest global official lender.

4.1 Financial stability implications of Fintech[11]

Fintech reduces costs and frictions, increases efficiency and competition, and broadens access to financial services. But this new organization of banks and other financial firms raises new regulatory challenges. Digital banks, also known as "neobanks," are growing in systemic importance in their local markets. Neobanks are fintech firms that offer software and other technologies to streamline mobile and online banking. They generally specialize in a limited number of products, such as checking and saving accounts. They also tend to be nimbler and transparent than their megabank counterparts, even though many of them partner with such institutions to insure their financial products.

Preliminary evidence suggests that neobanks take higher risks in retail credit originations without appropriate provisioning and that they underprice credit risk. They also take higher risks in securities portfolios and do not maintain sufficient liquidity.

By taking innovation to a new level, a form of financial intermediation based on crypto assets, known as decentralized finance (DeFi), has enjoyed extraordinary growth between 2020 and 2022. DeFi is increasingly interconnected with traditional financial intermediaries. While its market size is still relatively small, unregulated DeFi poses market, liquidity, and cyber risks, against a backdrop of legal uncertainties. The absence of centralized entities governing DeFi is a challenge for effective regulation and supervision. This challenge is amplified by the international nature of those institutions—a fact that requires the cooperation of regulatory and supervisory agencies across different jurisdictions. The 2022 Global Financial Stability Report recommends that regulation and supervision should focus on issuers of stable coins and centralized exchanges, and should encourage the development of industry codes of conduct and self-regulation.

4.2 Impact of the war in Ukraine on global financial vulnerabilities[12]

Russia's invasion of Ukraine is causing an intense humanitarian crisis. More than 12 million people are estimated to have been displaced and more than 13 million require urgent humanitarian assistance. Ukraine's economy is being devastated and the acute trauma suffered by the population will have enduring consequences. The

[11] This subsection draws on chapter 3 of the Global Financial Stability Report 2022 [12].

[12] This subsection draws freely on Ref. [15].

war in Ukraine has set back the global response to—and the recovery of the global economy from—the COVID-19 pandemic.

Prior to the invasion, the world was focused on the health and economic challenges caused by the pandemic. In particular, supporting the global economy amid an uneven recovery characterized by lingering supply bottlenecks; the withdrawal of policy support; and rising inflation, including for food and energy. The war has added a global adverse impact, especially through the prices of commodity markets. Russia is the world's largest exporter of wheat, accounting for 18% of global exports. Ukraine accounts for a further 7%. Russia is also the largest exporter of natural gas (25%), palladium (23%), nickel (22%), and fertilizers (14%). It also accounts for 18% of global exports of coal, 14% of platinum, 11% of crude oil, and 10% of refined aluminum.[13]

Europe's dependence on Russia for energy renders its economy vulnerable. Russian exports account for more than 35% of the euro area's imports of natural gas, more than 20% of oil, and 40% of coal (Figure 3.E in Ref. [16]). Russia is also dependent on the euro area for its exports, with around 40% of its crude oil and natural gas going to the euro area. While Russia may eventually be able to redirect some of its exports of gas and oil to others, this will be constrained by the existing pipeline infrastructure. Some emerging markets and developing economies (EMDEs) rely heavily on Russia and Ukraine for food and fertilizer. Russia and Ukraine account for more than 75% of imports of wheat in many countries. Logistics relating to transporting crops also remain a challenge; about 90% of Ukraine's grain trade flows through Black Sea ports that are currently blocked by the Russian navy. Russia has recommended that fertilizer manufacturers halt exports of fertilizer, which will hinder food production in parts of the world, since Russia is the largest exporter of fertilizers, accounting for 14% of global exports.

Although no global systemic event affecting financial institutions or markets has materialized so far, the war raised financial stability risks along several dimensions. Equity market volatility has risen markedly, especially in Europe. The European VSTOXX index shot up briefly in early March and remains unusually elevated. Equity volatility in the United States (as proxied by the VIX Index) also increased substantially in the month following the start of the war, though has since declined somewhat. Sovereign borrowing costs have increased since the start of the war. U.S. 10-year government bond yields have risen considerably, reflecting a range of factors including higher expected inflation.

Spreads on EMDE bonds have not widened significantly on average, although bond issuance by EMDEs across February–March was weaker than in the same period of any year since 2016. For some financial institutions, a recession in Russia is likely to result in substantial losses. Some European banks have material linkages with Russian entities facing severe losses, such as Sberbank. The majority of European banking exposures to Russia are through the claims of Russia-based subsidiaries, however, which are primarily funded by local creditors and depositors. Combined with the healthy capitalization of European banks prior to the war, this should reduce the probability of losses being amplified into European bank funding markets.

Nonetheless, large equity losses for exposed banks seem probable, as implied by drops in the equity prices of European banks perceived to be exposed to Russia following the introduction of sanctions. The profits and liquidity positions of

[13] Ukraine is the largest exporter of seed oils primarily used in cooking, accounting for two-fifths of global production, and is also the fourth largest exporter of corn, accounting for 13% of global exports. Ukraine also produces up to 50% of global neon gas, which is a critical element used in chip making.

institutional investors will also be impacted by write-downs on Russian assets with encumbered liquidity and by the need to hold additional margin against implicated exposures.

4.3 Implications of the rise in China's lending[14]

In contrast to global lending by advanced economies that originates in private banks and private capital markets, Chinese international lending originates in official sources. By 2017, China has become the largest official creditor surpassing the World Bank and the IMF. China has been lending to well over 100 countries. As of 2017, the highest ratio of official lending to local GDP was around 70% for Djibouti and about 6% for Ghana, which occupies the fiftieth place in this ranking (Figure 6 in Ref. [17]). The terms of Chinese official lending typically resemble those of commercial banks and about 50% of such loans to developing countries are not reported in standard debt statistics. Loans are denominated in USD or in local currencies. They are usually secured by means of domestic real assets or receipts owned by the borrower's country public or private entity that received the loan.

In case of default, the Chinese government takes over those assets. Essentially, potential financial difficulties are resolved directly through debt-to-equity swaps. It is probable that in some cases, Chinese authorities extend official loans to relatively risky ventures hoping that the borrowers will be unable to repay in order to expand China's control of world real resources. Although this is likely to be disliked by borrowing countries, these built-in debt-equity swaps reduce the likelihood of an open financial crisis triggered by defaults. On the other hand, the opaqueness of Chinese official lending statistics makes it difficult, if not impossible, to evaluate other potential risks embedded in those loans.

5. Concluding remarks

Through description and analysis, this chapter has illustrated the causes and the variety of mechanisms through which past financial crises erupted. Although all crises are ultimately associated with loss of confidence in the financial system and evaporation of liquidity, the nature of crises varies across time as well as across countries. Future surprises are inevitable, but the experience accumulated from past crises suggests that the following safeguards can reduce the probability of financial crises:

- Fiscal management should prevent excessive deficits from pushing the debt/GDP ratio to the vicinity of ranges that spook both domestic and international lenders pushing up interest rates on government debt and shortening its maturity. Although it is more difficult to achieve this recommendation in EMDEs, it is particularly relevant for them since they possess relatively smaller resources and have limited access to capital markets.

- Conduct monetary policy to maintain inflation not too far from the internationally accepted norm of inflation targeting. In view of huge past monetary expansions and the current inflation, this is not an easy task but, again, is more difficult to attain for EMDEs.

[14] This subsection draws on [17].

- Cross-border capital flows provide significant benefits but may generate or amplify shocks. The traditional IMF view has been that this problem can be handled by using flexible exchange rates as shock absorbers cum IT. However, due to insufficient internal discipline, in many EMDEs fixed rates or crawling pegs are used as nominal anchors. Such economies should hold sufficient stock of forex reserves for intervention purposes. Those measures could be supplemented by temporary or permanent taxes on short-term capital movements.[15]

- Regulators and supervisors should be given enough powers and independence to identify, ahead of time, systemic and other risks and to enforce measures that can mitigate them.

- In particular, the swift growth of fintech institutions has left many regulatory voids. Filling those empty spaces soon is essential to avoid financial crises triggered by insufficient regulation and supervision in this quickly expanding area.

[15] Research at the IMF recently explores those recommendations. See, for example, Ref. [18].

Author details

Alex Cukierman[1,2,3†]

1 Tel-Aviv University, Tel-Aviv, Israel

2 Reichman University, Herzeliya, Israel

3 CEPR, London, UK

*Address all correspondence to: alexcuk@tauex.tau.ac.il

† I benefitted from useful discussions with Joshua Aizenman.

References

[1] FDIC. The LDC debt crisis. In: Chapter 5 in History of the Eighties—Lessons for the Future, Volume I: An Examination of the Banking Crises of the 1980s and Early 1990s. Washington, DC: FDIC; 1997

[2] Sims J, Romero J. Latin American debt crisis of the 1980 [Internet]. 2013. Available from: https://www.federalreservehistory.org/essays/latin-american-debt-crisis [Accessed: July 2, 2022]

[3] Carson M, Clark J. Asian Financial Crisis; July 1997–December 1998 [Internet]. 2013. Available from: https://www.federalreservehistory.org/essays/asian-financial-crisis [Accessed: July 6, 2022]

[4] Corsetti G, Pesenti P, Roubini N. What caused the Asian currency and financial crisis? Japan and the World Economy. 1999;**11**:305-373

[5] van de Wiel I. The Russian Crisis 1998 [Internet]. 2013. Rabobank. Available from: https://economics.rabobank.com/publications/2013/september/the-russian-crisis-1998/ [Accessed: July 7, 2022]

[6] Federal Reserve Bank of Dallas, Southwest Economy. Brazil: The First Financial Crisis of 1999. [Internet]. 1999. Available from: https://www.dallasfed.org/~/media/documents/research/swe/1999/swe9902c.pdf [Accessed: July 8, 2022]

[7] van de Wiel I. The Argentine Crisis 2001/2002 [Internet]. 2013. Rabobank. Available from: https://economics.rabobank.com/publications/2013/august/the-argentine-crisis-20012002-/ [Accessed: July 9, 2022]

[8] Cukierman A. A retrospective on the subprime crisis and its aftermath ten years after Lehman's collapse. Economic Systems. 2019;**43**:100713. Available from: https://www.alexcuk.sites.tau.ac.il/_files/ugd/179175_2aa36725d06a4b2f97768455ebee99b0.pdf

[9] Fatas A. What has the Eurozone learned from the financial crisis? Harvard Business Review. 2018. Available from: https://hbr.org/2018/09/what-has-the-eurozone-learned-from-the-financial-crisis

[10] Cukierman A. Monetary policy and institutions before, during, and after the global financial crisis. Journal of Financial Stability. 2013;**9**:373-384. Available from: https://www.alexcuk.sites.tau.ac.il/_files/ugd/179175_54a002bc7f704b61aedab02bfe86da82.pdf?index=true

[11] Bernanke B. The Courage to Act: A Memoir of a Crisis and its Aftermath. NY: Norton and Company; 2015

[12] Global Financial Stability Report 2022. IMF. [Internet]. Available from: https://www.imf.org/en/Publications/GFSR/Issues/2022/04/19/global-financial-stability-report-april-2022 [Accessed: July 13, 2022]

[13] Deghi A, Natalucci F, Qureshi M. Emerging market Bank's government debt holdings pose financial stability risks. IMF Blog. 2022. Available from: https://blogs.imf.org/2022/04/18/emerging-market-banks-government-debt-holdings-pose-financial-stability-risks/ [Accessed: July 13, 2022]

[14] Han B. Original Sin Dissipation and Currency Exposures in Emerging Markets. International Department,

Bank of Korea. Available from: https://papers.ssrn.com/sol3/papers.cfm?abstract_id=4066583 [Accessed: July 25, 2022]

[15] Guenette JD, Kenworthy P, Wheeler C. Implications of the War in Ukraine for the Global Economy. 2022. Equitable Growth, Finance and Institutions Policy Note 3. World Bank Group. Available from: https://thedocs.worldbank.org/en/doc/5d903e848db1d1b83e0ec8f744e55570-0350012021/related/Implications-of-the-War-in-Ukraine-for-the-Global-Economy.pdf [Accessed: July 19, 2022]

[16] Bachmann R, Baqaee D, Bayer C, Kuhn M, Löschel A, Moll B, et al. What if? The Economic Effects for Germany of a Stop of Energy Imports from Russia. 2022. EconPol Policy Report 36, ifo Institute and Leibniz Institute for Economic Research at the University of Munich

[17] Horn S, Reinhart C, Trebesh C. China's overseas lending. Journal of International Economics. 2021;**133**. Available from: https://www.sciencedirect.com/science/article/pii/S0022199621001197 [Accessed: July 25, 2022]

[18] Basu S, Boz E, Gopinath G, Roch F, Unsal F. A Conceptual Model for the Integrated Policy Framework. 2020 IMF WP/20/121. [Internet]. https://books.google.co.il/books?hl=en&lr=&id=nrEaEAAAQBAJ&oi=fnd&pg=PA2&dq=imf+integrated+policy+framework&ots=rX9K1N7OIe&sig=4-sT84d_bzF_yQNkIL6O5Ln3ZRI&redir_esc=y#v=onepage&q=imf%20integrated%20policy%20framework&f=false [Accessed: July 20, 2022]

Chapter 5

Central Bank Transparency and Speculative Attacks: An Overview and Insights from a Laboratory Experiment in Tunisia

Emna Trabelsi

Abstract

We propose the use of experimental economics as an innovative tool to introduce economic issues. The basic game of the experiment is a simple beauty contest model by Morris and Shin. Precisely, the paper contributes to the continuous debate on the effect of transparency in a context of a speculative attack using an experimental approach. In the spirit of subsequent protocols of Heinemann et al. and Cornand such as a laboratory experiment is designed to test theoretical predictions of static coordination games, players have access to heterogeneous information sets and according to which they have to decide between a risky action whose payoff depends on the decision made by the other players, and a safe action that generates a fixed gain. Results indicate perfect coordination in 61.75% of the total situations. However, nonparametric tests reveal no evidence that players really differentiate between public and private information, and of a destabilizing effect of public information due to self-fulfilling beliefs. The findings have policy implications regarding optimal tools for information disclosure. We performed the experiment on students who do not have any previous knowledge about game theory or the context.

Keywords: speculative attack game, transparency, private information, public information, simulations, experimental economics, intrinsic motive

1. Introduction

Economic experiments are becoming increasingly popular as an innovative tool to introduce economic issues. Basically, they are used to test theoretical predictions derived from the game theory. In this paper, we give a special focus to the coordination games under heterogeneous information (public versus private) as sparked in the influential paper by Morris and Shin [1]. Such a category of games is considered as a "structure of economic decision problems" in the words of Heinemann et al. [2]. More precisely, speculative attacks on a currency peg can be modeled as a coordination game. With respect to the theoretical framework of Morris and Shin [1], central bank transparency stands for the precision of public information, but transparency, in general, includes also the precision of private information. Receiving different information in nature has consequences on agents' beliefs, which, in turn, impact the likelihood of a speculative attack occurrence: (see Trabelsi [3] for an econometric analysis). According to Morris and Shin [1], increasing the precision of public information is not always good, and generally leads to ambiguous effects on social welfare.[1]

Two main experiments that explore the use of private (specific to each agent) versus public information (observed by all) are by Heinemann et al. [2] and Cornand [5] who extends the analysis of the former to allow for signals of different nature. Szkup and Tervino [6] resume the experimental design of Heinemann et al. [2], but more precise private information is made available to agents at a certain cost. Costain et al. [7] conduct an experiment with a sequential move while previous actions are observed. They show that there is a specific region where the event of "all players attack" or "no play attacks" happens with a probability of more than 1%. Experiments on speculative attacks generalize the static setting to a dynamic one. For example, Cheung and Friedman [8] propose an entry game in continuous time. At each point in time, each player chooses to attack or not. The attack is made at a certain cost, which is cumulative as long as the player has attack status. Fehr et al. [9] make an important observation of sunspot equilibria when analyzing a coordination game of agents deciding between different assets and receiving noisy signals about them. Battiston and Harrison [10] suggest a novel approach that makes information about other players' behavior observable through a connected network. They find that information about sunspots improves coordination, while information about other players' behavior hampers it. Other works (See for instance Trabelsi and Hichri [11]) provide an experiment in a closer context by testing treatment of fragmented information (a common information per sub-group of agents) against a treatment of partial publicity (public information observed by a fraction of agents) that was introduced by Cornand and Heinemann [12]. Other experiments that apply coordination games can be found in Trautmann and Vlahu [13] to study strategic loan default. More recent studies complement this setting by analyzing information transmission in networks [14, 15].

Although the protocol is close to Cornand [5] – which has also been already inspired by the experimental design of Heinemann et al. [2] – three main differences (while the other parameters are kept the same) between our protocol and theirs are detected:

- The number of subjects (players) in the game;
- The use of a discrete uniform distribution of the true state and the signals for the sake of simplicity (See details in the main text of the following sections);
- The absence of real-monetary incentives.

Usually, economic experiments are computerized. The advantage of using fewer numbers of subjects allows us to perform the experiment by paper and pencil. Each player writes his or her own contribution on a sheet of paper. Interpreting the results with caution is, thus, appealing since the coordination games are sensitive to variation in the subjects' pool. Except the monetary incentive, all the conditions of implementing a standard laboratory experiment are respected. The experiment is run on students who do not know the context or the purpose previously.

1 For a succinct review of literature on the subject, we refer readers to Allegret and Cornand [4].

The fact that earnings (expressed in the Experimental Currency Unit) are not really paid is explained to the participants in advance. But to maintain interest, we passed out forms on which students can keep track of their hypothetical earnings [16]. Our experiment turns up an interesting attempt by applying the argument of Read [17] on the non-necessity of monetary payments in experimental economics. On p. 266, he asserts the following: "*My view is that monetary incentives are not an experimental magic bullet. They are one part of the experimentalist's arsenal [..]*". Read [17] concludes further that "*[...] there is no basis for requiring the use of real incentives to do experimental economics*". He departs from the fact that people have powerful intrinsic stimulations to do their best and money decreases their cognitive exertion. According to the same author, the use or not of monetary payments is akin to whether the objective of the experimenter is to arouse extrinsic or intrinsic motives of the players. In our case, we choose to make subjects rely on their intrinsic motives to play the game.

The rest of the paper is structured as follows; Section 2 describes the theoretical framework on which the experiment is based and Section 3 presents the experimental protocol. We discuss the main results in Section 4. We provide post-experiment discussion in Section 5 and Section 6 concludes.

2. Theoretical deliberations of the economic game

This section provides a theoretical background that motivates the economic game. First, based on the theoretical predictions of the game-theoretic model of Morris and Shin [1], we develop the framework that will be used in the experimental design. Then, within this framework, we derive the main results.

2.1 Speculative attack as a coordination game under heterogeneous information

Speculative attacks can be modeled as a coordination game with strategic complementarities. In the experiment, we employ a simple beauty contest model of Morris and Shin [1] with a finite number of economic agents N who decide simultaneously whether to attack or not.[2] Let us Y denote the fundamental state of the economy. The higher Y is, the better the state of the economy.

The gains of agents are given as follows:

- If an agent chooses to attack, he/she gets:
    - Y, if the proportion of agents who attach exceeds $a(Y)$.
    - 0, if the attack fails
- If an agent chooses to not attack, he/she gets a fixed reward equal to T.

Agents decide to attack or not based on two types of information (signals) given the state of the economy Y. Hence, the central bank disseminates posterior private and public information, where the public signal $Z/Y \rightarrow N\left(0, \sigma_\eta^2\right)$. Individually, they

[2] It is a concept developed by Keynes [18] to explain the fluctuations in equity markets. It is the view that much of investment is driven by the expectations about what other investors think, rather than expectations about the fundamental profitability.

receive private signals $x_i \rightarrow N(0, \sigma_\varepsilon^2)$. Morris and Shin [19] and Hellwig [20] show that there is a unique equilibrium with a critical state below which currency crisis occurs with certainty, that provided private information is sufficiently precise relative to the public information. Metz [21] showed that the signals' interaction may have adverse effects. Her theoretical predictions can be summarized as follows:

- If the state of the economy is bad ($Y\downarrow$) and the public information is more precise than the private signal, then an attack is likely to occur.
- If the state of the economy is good ($Y\uparrow$), more precise public information reduces the probability of an attack.

3. Experimental design matching theoretical model

3.1 Payoff function and signals

An unknown number Y is selected randomly from a range of values {10, 11..., 90}. Players do not know this number but have to guess it based on two types of information (signals). The first signal is public (Pu), common to all players in the same game session. The second is private (Pr). It is specific to each subject (player). Both signals are randomly selected from the same interval [Y-10, Y + 10]. The decision consists of choosing between a safe action A that brings a fixed payoff T or a risky action B that generates a payoff Y under certain conditions:

- If a player chooses a secure action **A**, he/she earns T =
    - 20 in stage 1 of sessions 1 and 2 and in stage 2 of sessions 3–5
    - 50 in stage 2 of sessions 1 and 2 and in stage 1 of sessions 3–5
- If a player chooses a risky action **B**, he/she earns:
    - **Y,** in these cases:

If the unknown number Y is in the interval	Then at least ... of the participants have to select B in order to have a positive gain
[10,39]	3
[40,59]	2
[60,90]	1

- **0**, otherwise.

3.2 Treatment and session description

A sole treatment of Morris and Shin [1] (hereafter MS) is implemented for this exercise. The treatment consists of 2 stages. Each stage comprises 8 periods (The stages differ only by the amount allocated to the choice of a safe action A). In each period and for each of the 10 situations, 3 participants have to decide between a safe action A that generates a fixed gain (T = 20 in stage 1 and T = 50 in stage 2) and a risky action B whose payoff depends on two factors: The value of the true state Y and the choice of the participants playing in a game session. This game is repeated twice (Sessions 1–2). For sessions 3–5, the participants undergo the same game but we reverse the stages' order: in stage 1, T = 50, and in stage 2, T = 20 (cf. **Table 1**).

3.3 Procedural considerations

The experiment was carried out at the Higher Institute of Management of Tunis. The simulations were run using R.2.0.6 software. The 15 subjects who participated in this experiment were split into 5 groups (N = 5). Five sessions were devoted to one treatment of MS, producing a total of five independent observations per treatment.

Subjects are inexperienced students from the unit of applied and quantitative analysis (UAQUAP) switched to the social and economic policy analysis laboratory (SEPAL) and from the laboratory of operational research, decision and process control (LARODEC), both located at the Higher Institute of Management in Tunisia. Sessions lasted about one hour and a half. In each period and for each of the 10 situations, subjects have to make a decision on the true state Y given the signals.

The procedure was kept the same throughout the experiment. Three subjects were seated apart so communication was not possible. The same group of three individuals played for 16 periods. At each individual's place, there was an instruction sheet, one response table and a piece of scrap paper on which subjects can take notes about their choices after each decision and information phase. Instructions (given in detail in Appendix A) were distributed in written form (in French) to the subjects and were read out loud before the beginning of each session. It was made sure that these instructions were well understood. Subjects were asked to raise their hands if they had any questions, and answers were given privately by the experimenter (See Appendix B for details and **Table 2** for an example). To make sure that players understand the game rules, a quiz was distributed to the participants at the beginning of each session.[3]

4. Results

The raw data are available upon request from the author. In what follows, we use non-parametric tests and logistic regressions in order to analyze our results.[4]

4.1 Some general considerations about individuals' behavior

4.1.1 Existence of threshold strategies

According to Heinemann et al. [2], the behavior is consistent with undominated strategy if this behavior, during a period, is consistent with the existence of thresholds.

In other terms,

- B is dominated by A if $\max(x_i, Z) < T-\varepsilon$
- A is dominated by B if $\min(x_i, Z) > T+\varepsilon$

[3] See Appendix C.

[4] All tables and figures related to our results are available in Appendix D.

Figure 1 displays the number of cases where subjects played undominated strategies. This is very predominant especially in the sixth and twelfth periods, with 65 and 62 cases in total, respectively. More generally, a threshold strategy means that subjects were not able to predict sometimes others' choices.

Although signals differ in nature (public versus private), different interpretations of public information lead somewhat to this common information to be a private one. Consequently, common information does not lead necessarily to common knowledge. In other terms, different interpretations of public information are considered also as private ones.

Given the fact that the number of players is low, the level of reasoning of players increases sometimes but with strategies change.

4.1.2 The determinant signal of individual behavior

We estimate the probability with which a subject chooses B by fitting a logistic distribution function to observed choices. The cumulative logistic distribution is given by:

$$P(B) = \frac{1}{1 + \exp(-a - bPr - cPu).}$$

We analyse whether the public signal is used as a focal point by the subjects. We define the null hypothesis as follows:

H0: the weight assigned to the public signal (c) is not different from the weight assigned to the private signal (b).

We test H0 owing to a Wilcoxon matched pairs signed rank test and both of them allowed us to derive these observations:

- Players seem to be indifferent between the two types of signals. P-value is equal to 0.9594. So, there is no evidence of using public information as a focal point by the agents. In other terms, subjects give equal weights to both signals (cf. **Table 3**).

4.2 The threshold to successful attacks

Players have a tendency to choose the safe action (A) for low values of Y and to decide on the risky action (B) for higher values of Y (cf. **Figure 2**).

Table 4 gives an indication on states in which B was a successful strategy. We define the interval of indeterminacy; whose lower bound is the lowest value of Y and above which the attack is successful, and whose upper bound is the highest value of Y until which B fails. The middle point of that interval gives information about the probability of a successful attack and the amplitude of this interval indicates the predictability of a successful attack.

4.3 Probability and the predictability of a speculative attack

4.3.1 The aggregate behavior analysis

4.3.1.1 Probability of a successful attack

Table 5 displays some statistics relative to the probability and the predictability of an attack. The mean threshold to success, as well as the average width of an interval of indeterminacy, is higher when the gain associated with the safe action increases (T = 50). That observation coincides with OLS estimations.[5] We tested the impact of control variables (cf. **Table 6** for description and definition of data) on mean thresholds Y* through linear regression (Eq. 1).

$$Y_i^* = \gamma_0 + \gamma_1 T_i + \gamma_2 Ord_i + \gamma_3 TO_i + u_i \quad (1)$$

Y* is the threshold state that characterizes the behavior of a player (an agent) who attacks if he/she "*gets a signal above this threshold, and does not attack otherwise*" ([7], p.2). The payoff associated with the safe action T has a significant and positive impact on the probability of an attack. Order (Ord) adds a high and significant value to the level of threshold. An interaction term is used to control for nonlinearity in the payoff function. The variable TO is included to capture the different sizes of the order effect in the two stages. It is negative but insignificant. Overall, the controls explain about 89% of the total regression.

4.3.1.2 Predictability of an attack

We regress the interval that separates between the highest state up to which action B always failed and the lowest state from which action B was always successful (ΔY^*) on some controls.

$$\Delta Y_i^* = \gamma_0 + \gamma_1 T_i + \gamma_2 Ord_i + \gamma_3 TO_i + u_i \quad (2)$$

Eq. (3) in **Table 7** shows that only order variable (Ord) has a significant impact on ΔY^*.

4.3.2 The individual behavior analysis

The results of individual behavior analysis are in accordance with those of aggregate behavior. We estimate the proportion of agents who choose a risky action B by using a logistic estimation, for each session as follows:

To estimate the probability of choosing an action B, we use a logit model:

$$P(De) = \frac{1}{1 + \exp(-De)}$$

The relationship between De and the independent variables is supposed to be linear:

$$De = a + b\ Pr + c\ Pu + u, u \text{ is the error term}$$

$$\text{Mean} = -a/(b + c) \text{ and standard deviation} = \pi/(b + c)\sqrt{3}.$$

The mean of the function ($-a/(b + c)$) is an indication of the probability of an attack and its standard deviation ($\pi/(b + c)\sqrt{3}$) measures the predictability of a speculative attack (cf. **Table 8**).

The **results** can be interpreted in two ways:

---

5 Following Heinemann et al. [2], as the individual behavior does not change after the first periods, we combine data of the last four periods in order to improve the quality of the estimates.

i. The estimated probability that players choose B is conditional on Y and x_i, respectively;

ii. The estimation of individual thresholds;

As in our previous findings, the mean of thresholds is higher when T = 50 (cf. **Table 9**), but the standard deviation of thresholds is lower when the payoff is lower.

4.3.2.1 Probability of a successful attack

Eq. (3) estimates the effect of control variables on the estimated mean threshold.

$$-a/(b+c) = \gamma_0 + \gamma_1 T_i + \gamma_2 Ord_i + \gamma_3 TO_i + u_i \quad (3)$$

The payoff of the secure action contributes significantly and positively to the estimated mean threshold. The result is in accordance with the preliminary analysis following **Table 9**. Order effect is negative and significant. The interaction term (TO) is, however, insignificant.

4.3.2.2 Predictability of an attack

It is clear that the average standard deviation is always higher when the payoff of the secure action is high.

$$\pi/(b+c)\sqrt{3} = \gamma_0 + \gamma_1 T_i + \gamma_2 Ord_i + \gamma_3 TO_i + u_i \quad (4)$$

Eq. (4) shows that this is indeed significant only at 10%. The interaction term (TO) regains its significance but the order variable (Ord) turns out to be insignificant although it has its expected sign.

4.4 Coordination failure

In this section, we study the impact of the informational structure on coordination. We distinguish two extreme cases: Perfect coordination versus total coordination failure.

We define perfect coordination as the situation in which all agents choose the same action. Total coordination failure is the situation in which two players choose the same action. There are a total of 494 cases where subjects played the same action (cf. **Table 10**).[6] Following Cornand [5], a deep interpretation of the coordination concept can be observed through a measure of the former (i.e., number of regrettable decisions). Indeed, when individual behavior fails, this means that the subject had difficulty in interpreting the signals he/she received. Therefore, he/she was unable to predict whether an attack was successful or not. This can happen in two situations:

i. He/she chose B and the gain =0 (failed attack)

ii. He/she chose A while B would have brought a higher payoff (a missed opportunity to attack)

[6] Total number of situations = 10*16*5 = 800.

We proceed to calculate the number of regrettable decisions (the player regrets his choice according to the situations described above). **Figure 3** shows that this number is particularly high in the first periods (periods 2 and 3) of stage 1. The number of regrettable decisions decreases over the following periods and regains a higher peak – though a bit lower than in periods 2 and 3 – at the end of stage 1 (period 8). Overall, the number of regrettable decisions clearly decreases in stage 2.

5. Post experiment discussion

As mentioned earlier, students had no knowledge of game theory or of experimental economics. Most of them have majors in Finance, Economics, and Management Applied Computer Sciences. At each session's end, we begin the discussion by introducing (briefly) the theoretical background, which involves three topics and explain them in a simple manner:

- First of all, we presented to the students the structure of the game as **an economic decision problem** in the real world. Hence, they know that the instructor plays the role of the central bank as a provider of public information, while subjects represent the speculators (economic agents). The unknown number Y fits the state of the economy. The private signal x_i (Pr) represents the insider information about Y. It could correspond to any information that an individual has observed, such as news received through private discussions. The second signal Z (Pu) is commonly shared by all agents. The public signal can represent information gleaned from newspaper articles or other sources that report on central bank procedures.

- Given the game structure is clear for all students, we moved to the performance analysis. They observe that their own gains depend not only on their self-beliefs but also on their beliefs about other players' actions. Furthermore, they realize that the other players' behavior also relies on their own actions and so on. This is the most important feature of the **beauty contest game**.

- Students capture the idea that when the state of the economy (Y) was bad (let us say less than 50 and that they are in the stage where the payoff of a safe action brings 50), then **rational behavior** would follow a secure action A rather than a risky action B even if the attack was successful.

- Students confirmed that they relied on their **intrinsic motives** to learn a new and novel tool (i.e., experimental economics) although they did not engage for external rewards such as real monetary payments, but because they found the experimental game interesting and gratifying. This makes our learning challenge more successful than when the topic is explored through classical courses.

6. Concluding remarks

We presented an experiment with application on the role of transparency in currency crisis models. The originality of our contribution stems from the fact that such an exercise has never been implemented (to our knowledge) as a usual laboratory economic game with a pedagogical objective afterwards: (see Holt and Tanga [16], Alba-Frenandez et al. [22]). We find that public information plays somewhat a role in subjects' choices, but could not be considered obviously as a focal point in determining their decisions. Overall, transparency as measured by the precision of public information gives the central bank more control over traders' beliefs. However, the ability of the central bank to predict an attack is reduced as the traders get private information (uncontrolled by the central bank) from other sources. We further note that this experiment is a "première" in Tunisia. All published or unpublished (few) papers in the literature are about experiments conducted after ours. This adds value to our contribution and encourages us to carry out further economic experiments in our country about other scientific research objectives.

Acknowledgements

The author is thankful to the students of the Higher Institute of Management of Tunis for their participation to the experiment, to Camille Cornand for the feedback after the work's realization and to Prof. Razali Haron for useful comments.

Appendices

A.1 General instructions (Translation of the French instructions)

Today, you will participate in an experiment. Your gain will depend upon your decision and the decisions of other participants in your group.

Since your gains depend on the decisions that you will make during the experiment, it is important to understand the instructions. Read them carefully. If you have any questions, raise your hand and the experimenter will come to your desk and provide answers.

Your main task

You and **2** other individuals are asked to choose between a safe action (**A**) and a risky action (**B**) for each of the **10** situations in the Table. All you have to do is to submit **A** or **B**. Gains will be determined by the following two factors:

- The true value **Y;**
- The actions (**A** or **B**) chosen by the others.

At the time when you make your decisions, you will not know either of these two factors. You will not know the decision made by your two other playmates because your playmates are deciding at the same time as you. You will not know the value of the true state **Y** because you have to make your decision before this one is revealed. Therefore, you will need to decide based on the information that will be made available to you.

Guessing the true state Y

At the beginning of each period, you and the **2** participants in your session will receive two signals that will provide you with information about the true state **Y**. Both signals are randomly drawn given the true state from the interval [**Y**-10, **Y** + 10]. Because signals are randomly drawn, it is impossible to precisely predict the true state **Y** given the signals. However, they will give you an idea of a range where the true state **Y** might be. The examples below show you how signals should be interpreted:

Example 1

- The *public (common)* signal drawn for all the **3** participants is **54**, and then every participant will know that the true state **Y** will be between 44 and 64.
- Suppose that you received a *private signal* **60**. On top of that, you know that the true state **Y** is between 50 and 70.

Based on both signals, you can deduce that the true state **Y** is between **50 and 64**.

Example 2

- The *public (common)* signal drawn for all the **3** participants is **5**, then every participant will know that the true state **Y** will be between 10 and 15.
- Suppose that you received it as a *private signal* **12**. On top of that, you know that the true state **Y** is between 10 and 22.

Based on both signals, you can deduce that the true state **Y** is between **10 and 15. Reminder:** The value **Y** cannot be less than 10!

Guessing the action of your playmates

In the previous section, we explained how to guess the true state given the information that you receive (*public* and *private*). However, your gain will depend also on how well you can guess the actions chosen by the **2** other participants. The decisions of others are made by humans; therefore, your best option would be to try to predict the action the other participants are going to decide given their information. Here is what you know and what you do not know about the information available to other players in your group:

- They receive **2** signals, just like you do;
- You know the first signal that everyone receives. It is *public* (*common*). All players in your session will have the same signal.

- You do not know the second signal that they receive. The second signal is a *private* signal. It means that you cannot see private signals received by the two other players. It also means that they cannot see the private signal that you receive.

- You do know that the private signals of other players are generated in the same way as your private signal. Most importantly that they are also centred around the true state **Y**. Use your knowledge about the information that other players have to predict the action they will choose (**A** or **B**). Based on that, you can make your final decision for each of the **10** situations.

A.2 Instructions relative to the first stage of the MS treatment (the two stages differ only by the gain associated with the choice of action A)

For each of the 10 situations, a number **Y** is drawn randomly from a discrete uniform distribution {10, 11, 12 … ., 90}. This number is the same for all **3** participants. When you make your choice, you will not know the true value of **Y** until you decide.

Your gain

As explained above, your earnings depend upon the information you receive and the action you choose:

- If you choose **A**, you earn T = 20.

- If you choose **B**, you earn:

- **Y**, in these cases:

If the unknown number Y is in the interval	Then at least … of the participants have to select B in order to have a positive gain
[10,39]	3
[40,59]	2
[60,90]	1

- **0**, otherwise.

A.3 Training questions (before the game starts)

A.3.1 Training questions (Sessions 1–2)

Tick the right answer

1- During a situation of a certain period, you receive 2 signals: Public (common) signal = 45, private signal = 38, then **Y** is:	a. between 35 and 48 ☐ b. between 28 and 48 ☐ c. between 35 and 55 ☐
2- At **stage 1** and during the first **8** periods, you choose a safe action **A**, then your gain is:	a. 20 ☐ b. 50 ☐

3- How many periods will you play during the game?	a. 8 ☐ b. 16 ☐

A.3.2 Training questions (Sessions 3–5)

Tick the right answer

1- During a situation of a certain period, you receive 2 signals: Public (common) signal = 40, private signal = 32, then **Y** is:	a. between 22 and 42 ☐ b. between 30 and 42 ☐ c. between 30 and 50 ☐
2- At **stage 1** and during the first **8** periods, you choose a safe action **A**, then your gain is:	a. 20 ☐ b. 50 ☐
3- How many periods will you play during the game?	a. 8 ☐ b. 16 ☐

A.4 List of Figures and Tables

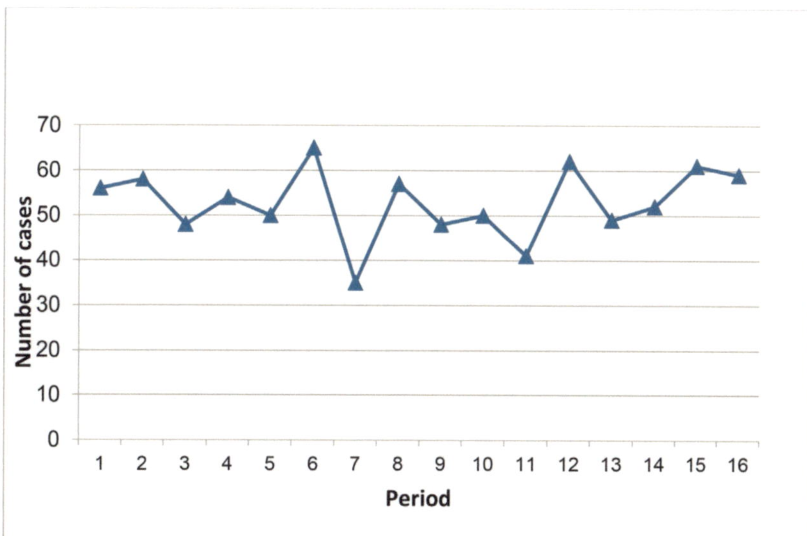

Figure 1.
Number of cases where behavior is consistent with undominated strategies.

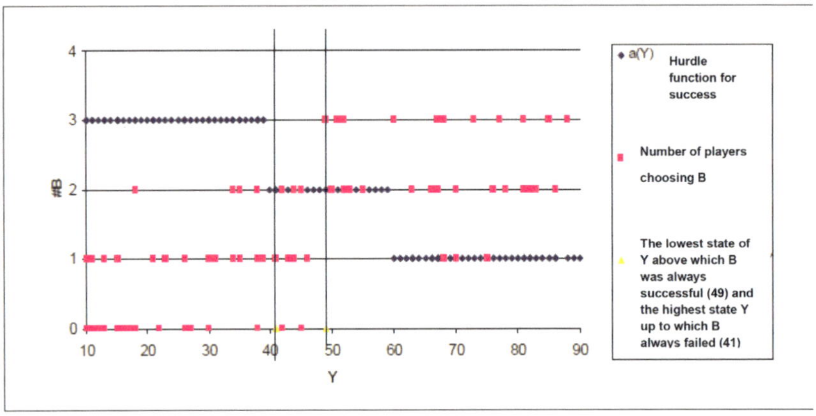

Figure 2.
Combined data from all 8 periods of one stage of a session. There are 80 values of Y selected in one stage. Dots indicate the number of subjects who played B. The hurdle function a(Y) is the minimal number of players needed for getting a reward while playing B. Dots below the hurdle function indicate states at which there was no successful attack. Dots on or above the hurdle function indicate successful attacks. Two points indicate the highest state up to which action B always failed and the lowest state from which B was always successful.

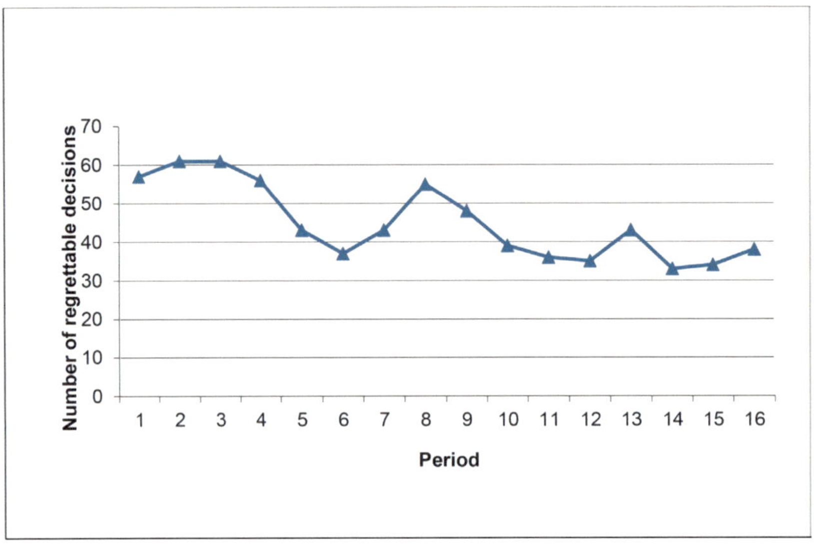

Figure 3.
Evolution of coordination.

Sessions	Treatment	Players per session	Stages	Periods
1–2	MS	3	1- T = 20	8
			2- T = 50	8
3–5	MS	3	1- T = 50	8
			2- T = 20	8
Total players			15	

Table 1.
Experiment: Summary.

Situation	Pr (x_i)	Pu (Z)	Choice	Y	Gain
1	36	41			
2	52	57			
3	22	27			
4	20	21			
5	41	29			
6	53	59			
7	19	19			
8	3	3			
9	82	81			

Note: Each period is divided into a decision phase and an information phase. In the decision phase, each participant receives a table containing 10 situations of the true state Y. When all participants made their choices, the decision phase is finished and an information phase begins, where the value of Y is indicated for each situation your own decision and your gain. After the players return their papers, a new period begins and participants cannot see the information from the previous period. Nevertheless, they are allowed to take notes.

Table 2.
Example of a paper sheet received by a player during a certain round of the game (T = 20).

b	c	c-b	sign
0.11	0.08	−0.03	(−)
0.12	0.2	0.08	(+)
0.05	0.01	−0.04	(−)
0.03	0.08	0.05	(+)
0.06	0.07	0.01	(+)
0.14	0.12	−0.02	(−)
0.09	0.01	−0.08	(−)
0.07	0.08	0.01	(+)
0.08	−0.02	−0.1	(−)
−0.02	0.34	0.36	(+)

Note: number of positive differences = 5.

Table 3.
Wilcoxon matched pairs signed rank test.

Session	T = 20	T = 50
1 20/50	40–60	52–67
2 20/50	41–49	49–61
3 50/20	33–40	52–59
4 50/20	39–43*	53–60
5 50/20	39–49	53–65

Note: **indicates sessions where states with successful and failed attacks can be clearly divided.*

Table 4.
Indeterminacy interval.

MS Treatment	T = 20	T = 50
Mean threshold to success (Y^*)	43.3	57.1
Average width of the interval of indeterminacy (ΔY^*)	9.8	10.6
Standard deviation	4.45	1.83
Number of sessions	5	5

Table 5.
Observed mean threshold to success and an average width of the interval between the highest state, up to which action B always failed and the lowest state from which, action B is always successful.

Notation	Nature	Definition	
T	*dummy*	0: *payoff* of the safe action T = 20	1: T = 50
Ord(er)	*dummy*	0: session beginning with T = 50	1: session beginning with T = 20
TO	*dummy*	0: if Ord = 0 or T = 20	1: if Ord = 1 and T = 50
De (cision)	*dummy*	0: if a player chooses A	1: if a player chooses B
Ri(sk)	integer	Number of agents who are not risk-averse	
x_i	integer	Private signal in sessions (MS)	
Z	integer	Public signal in sessions (MS)	
Y^*	real	Middle point between the highest value of Y above which action B failed and the lowest value of Y above which B is always a successful strategy.	
ΔY^*	integer	Indeterminacy interval width	
$-a/(b+c)$	real	Estimated mean threshold	
$\pi/(b+c)\sqrt{3}$	real	Estimated standard deviation of thresholds	

Table 6.
Definition of variables.

N°	# observations	Independent variables: Coefficients				R^2
		Constant	T	Ord	TO	R^2 adjusted
1	10	40.5***	14.5***	7**	−4.75	0.89
		(29.64)	(5.73)	(2.47)	(−1.19)	0.83
2	10	7**	1.67	7*	−2.17	0.44
		(2.82)	(0.47)	(1.78)	(0.39)	0.16
3	10	37.65***	16.24***	11.34**	−6.17	0.85
		(14.74)	(4.5)	(2.81)	(−1.08)	0.77
4	10	8.25*	12.53*	11.64	−21.34*	0.41
		(1.67)	(1.8)	(1.49)	(−1.93)	0.13

*Note: t-student statistics are between (). *, **, *** denote statistical significance at 10%, 5%, 1%, respectively.*

Table 7.
Results of the estimation by MCO.

N° session	Stage	Information	Order	*payoff T*	Estimated parameters*			Estimated mean	Estimated standard deviation
					a	b	c	$-a/(b+c)$	$\pi/(b+c)\sqrt{3}$
1	1	MS	20/50	20	−9.94	0.11	0.08	52.32	9.55
1	2	MS	20/50	50	−19.62	0.12	0.20	61.31	5.67
2	1	MS	20/50	20	−2.74	0.05	0.01	45.67	30.23
2	2	MS	20/50	50	−6.25	0.03	0.08	56.82	16.49
3	1	MS	50/20	50	−6.55	0.06	0.07	50.38	13.95
3	2	MS	50/20	20	−8.27	0.14	0.12	31.81	6.98
4	1	MS	50/20	50	−5.63	0.09	0.01	56.30	18.14
4	2	MS	50/20	20	−5.68	0.07	0.08	37.87	12.09
5	1	MS	50/20	50	−3.30	0.08	−0.02	55.00	30.23
5	2	MS	50/20	20	−13.85	−0.02	0.34	43.28	5.67

Note: Estimated parameters are based on the last four periods of each stage.

Table 8.
Results of logistic regressions.

MS Treatment	T = 20	T = 50
Average estimated mean *thresholds*	42.19	55.96
Average estimated standard deviation of *thresholds*	12.9	16.9
Number of sessions	5	5

Table 9.
Average estimated means and standard deviations of individual threshold to action B.

Sessions	Perfect coordination	Total coordination failure
MS	61.75%	38.25%

Table 10.
Percentage of situations in which all subjects played the same action (perfect coordination) and in which 1 or 2 played the same action (total coordination failure).

Jel Classification

C93, D82, F3

Author details

Emna Trabelsi[1,2]

1 Faculty of Economic and Management Sciences of Sousse, University of Sousse, Cité Riadh, Tunisia

2 SEPAL Laboratory, University of Tunis, Higher Institute of Management of Tunis, le Bardo, Tunisia

*Address all correspondence to: emna.trabelsi2007@yahoo.fr

References

[1] Morris S, Shin HS. The social value of public information. American Economic Review. 2002;**92**:1521-1534

[2] Heinemann F, Nagel R, Ockenfels P. The theory of global games on test: Experimental analysis of coordination games with public and private information. Econometrica. 2004;**72**: 1583-1599

[3] Trabelsi E. Does asymmetric information play a role in explaining the Asian crisis? Application to Indonesian and Malaysian cases using a two-state Markov Switching model. Economics Bulletin. 2011;**31**(1):560-571

[4] Allegret JP, Cornand C. The pros and cons of higher transparency: the case of speculative attacks. Recherches Économiques de Louvain/Louvain Economic Review. 2006;**72**(3):215-246

[5] Cornand C. Speculative attack and informational structure: An experimental study. Review of International Economics. 2006;**14**(5): 797-817

[6] Szkup, M, Trevino I. "Costly information acquisition in a speculative attack: Theory and experiments." Mimeo. 2013. Available from: https://econweb.ucsd.edu/~itrevino/pdfs/szkup_trevino_exp_july15.pdf

[7] Costain James S, Heinemann F, Ockenfels P. Multiple outcomes of speculative behavior in theory and in the laboratory. Mimeo. 2007. Available from: https://www.macroeconomics.tu-berlin.de/fileadmin/fg124/heinemann/papers/expt-070630.pdf

[8] Cheung Y-W, Friedman D. Speculative attacks: A laboratory study in continuous time. Journal of International Money and Finance. 2009; **28**(6):1064-1082

[9] Fehr D, Heinemann F, Llorente-Saguer A. The power of sunspots: An experimental analysis. Journal of Monetary Economics. 2019;**103**:123-136

[10] Battiston P., Harrisson, Sharon G. Believe or not: Experimental evidence on sunspot equilibria with social networks. Mimeo, 2022. Available from: https://celss.iserp.columbia.edu/sites/default/files/content/documents/Working%20Papers/battiston%20harrison%20sunspot.pdf

[11] Trabelsi E, Hichri W. Central bank transparency with (semi-)public information: Laboratory experiments. Journal of Behavioral and Experimental Economics. 2021;**90**:101645

[12] Cornand C, Heinemann F. Optimal degree of public information. The Economic Journal. 2008;**118**(528): 718-742

[13] Truatmann ST, Vhlau R. Strategic loan defaults and coordination: An experimental Analysis. Journal of Banking & Finance. 2013;**37**(3):747-760

[14] Currarini S, Feri F, Melendez-Jiménez MA. An experimental study on information sharing networks. 2015. Available from: http://www.hec.unil.ch/documents/seminars/deep/1612.pdf

[15] Galeotti A, Ghiglino C, Squintani F. Strategic information transmission in networks. Journal of Economic Theory. 2013;**148**:1751-1769

[16] Holt Charles A., Tanga Mc Daniel. Experimental economics in the classroom. 1996. Available from: http://people.virginia.edu/~cah2k/clasextr.pdf

[17] Read D. Monetary incentives, what are they good for? Journal of Economic Methodology. 2005;**12**(2):265-276

[18] Keynes JM. General Theory of Employment, Interest and Money. Cambridge University Press; 1936. p. 407

[19] Morris S, Shin HS. Global games: Theory and applications. In: Dewatripont M, Hansen L, Turnovsky S, editors. Advances in Economics and Econometric: The Eighth World Congress. Cambridge, MA: Cambridge University Press; 2003. pp. 56-114

[20] Hellwig C. Public information, private information and the multiplicity of equilibria in coordination games. Journal of Economic Theory. 2002;**107**: 191-222

[21] Metz CE. Private and public information in self-fulfilling currency crises. Journal of Economics. 2002;**76**: 65-85

[22] Alba-Fernandez V, Branas-Garza P, Jiménez-Jiménez F, Rodero-Cosano J. Teaching nash equilibrium and dominance: A classroom experiment on the beauty contest. Journal of Economic Education. 2006;**37**(3):305-322

Chapter 6

Asymmetric TVP-VAR Connectedness Approach: The Case of South Africa

Lethiwe Nzama, Thanda Sithole and Sezer Bozkus Kahyaoglu

Abstract

This chapter assesses connectedness of critical financial variables within the South African context. The key variables determining countries' international financial risk levels are the prices of their main export goods in the international markets. From this perspective, there is a connection between the prices of financialised commodities and precious metals in international markets, the exchange rates of the countries supplying these goods to the world economy and their risk indicators. As a result, a spill-over effect of financial risk increases the stress between the price movements in international markets, especially in countries whose national economy is based on the precious metals in question, and the risk indicators in international markets. From this point of view, the connection firstly between the gold prices (and secondly between platinum prices), which have an impact on the world economy, and the credit default swaps (CDSs), which show the country's risk level, and exchange rates of South Africa (RD) are examined. New econometric techniques are used for analysis based on the relevant literature. The empirical findings obtained from the study will be a source of information in the process of forming the economic policy of South Africa.

Keywords: gold and platinum prices, CDS, rand/dollar exchange rate, spillover, time-varying vector autoregressive (TVPVAR) model, dynamic connectedness, asymmetric connectedness, risk management, South Africa

1. Introduction

South Africa is a critical player in the global commodities. It is the largest producer (exporter) of global platinum [1]. In addition, South Africa is the eighth global producer of gold and, notably, the third largest in terms of global gold reserves, after Australia and Russia. Furthermore, the rand is one of the most traded emerging market currencies and, globally, among the top 20 [2, 3]. Understanding how it is integrated with commodities is crucial, considering the sovereign risk premium. Subsequently, this chapter studies the network connectedness of the dollar-denominated commodity (gold and platinum) prices, South Africa's rand exchange rate, and sovereign risk premium proxied by credit default swaps spread (CDS).

The connectedness of financial variables has increasingly become more critical for financial market participants and policymakers alike, especially after the 2007–2009 global financial crisis (GFC). Antonakakis et al. [4] echo this view and highlight that investigating the propagation of the financial crisis into the economy has been at the epicentre of academic research in recent years, especially in the aftermath of the GFC. Therefore, to provide insights into the financial market participants (and policymakers alike) interested in investing in South Africa, it is critical to understand the dynamic connectedness of commodities and currency accounting for the country's risk premium, as proposed here. Mensi et al. [5] argue that the growing cross-market information transmission in economic activities has amplified the contagion spillover and vulnerability of markets to external shocks. This provides context as to why studying the dynamic connectedness of financial networks is crucial.

To investigate how integrated our network is, we apply a Time-Varying Parameter–Vector Autoregressive (TVP-VAR) Connectedness Approach advanced by Antonakakis et al. [4] which was initially proposed by Diebold and Yilmaz [6]. This approach allows us to capture better the connectedness dynamics within the network of our selected financial variables. Several empirical studies have assessed the connectedness of commodities and exchange rate markets. A recent study by Mensi et al. [5], which extends from Antonakakis and Kizys [7], investigates volatility spillover, connectedness, and quantile dependence between precious metals and developed market currencies. Generally, their results reveal dynamic spillovers across precious metals and currencies and their respective connection with significant world events. However, their study does not include South Africa.

The most relevant recent study by Sayed and Charteris [3] investigates whether metals, grains, and energy commodities influence the South African rand and its volatility. They find a high degree of interconnectedness between the rand and commodities. Nevertheless, while their study is a good reference for our study, it does not account for the sovereign risk premium, which can provide further details in analysing the connectedness of the rand and commodities. In addition, our study is framed within an asymmetric time-varying setting, while their study uses a Dynamic Conditional Correlation-Generalised Autoregressive Conditional Heteroskedastic setting. Therefore, our study's contribution reflects both the time-varying connectedness approach and the inclusion of the CDS in the commodity-currency connectedness analysis in the case of South Africa.

The CDS spread can be used as a proxy for the sovereign credit risk profile, inferring those large spikes in CDS spread imply increased riskiness of sovereign assets, as investors demand high-risk premia to compensate for increased default risk [8]. Numerous studies have considered the connectedness of financial assets and CDS. Studies on the determinants of CDS have advanced two compelling reasons: firstly, financial integration and demand growth for sovereign CDS and secondly, investors' perception of higher credit risk and variability in emerging rather than developed markets [9]. Using Principal Component Analysis, de Boyri and Pavlova [9] find that global financial market factors are important drivers of sovereign CDS variability for the BRICS and MIST countries. Simonyan and Bayraktar [10] study the asymmetric dynamics in sovereign CDS pricing for a group of 11 emerging markets, including South Africa, and find some specific idiosyncratic and external factors (VIX and oil price) crucially affect CDS asymmetrically. Therefore, the CDS spread is crucial for financial market participants (and policymakers alike); so, we include it in our commodity-currency connectedness study for South Africa.

We focus on South Africa exclusively because of its global position within the African continent and its importance in the global commodities markets. In addition, we concur with Sayed and Charteris [3] that a single country study can provide great insights not identifiable in multiple country studies. Generally, we find a higher degree of interconnectedness within the network throughout the sample period. In addition, dynamic total connectedness is visibly responsive to some critical economic events, notably between 2014, 2016 and 2018.

The remainder of this chapter is organised in the following way: Section 2 provides a brief literature review on interconnectedness between financial variables, and network connectedness. Section 3 provides brief information about the data and details about the asymmetric TVP-VAR econometric model. Section 4 presents empirical findings, and Section 5 provides conclusions, as well as policy recommendations.

2. Literature review

In the literature, the real business cycle in the world has been analysed within the framework of world trade and world output. However, financial flows in the world economy have brought up the question of whether the global financial cycle is suitable for this, as well as analyses based on this real business cycle. In this regard, studies have begun to take into account the relationship between commodity prices, asset prices and financial risk indicators. In these studies, not only the real business cycle, but also the financial cycle and financial risk channels in this context were revealed. Thus, the sensitivity of the financial cycle to the relationship between commodity, asset and risk indicators is shown [11, 12]. In this study, the relations developed based on the aforementioned literature were analysed on a country basis within the framework of the asymmetric connectedness approach.

Various empirical publications have contributed to the investigation of global financial variable connectedness. Chatziantoniou et al. [13] apply the TVP-VAR Connectedness Approach to study interlinkages within a network of six major crude oil benchmarks[1]. Their study [13] found that the crude oil market exhibits a relatively high degree of co-movement with overall dynamic connectedness staying persistently above the 50% mark from May 14th, 1996, to December 3rd, 2020. Li et al. [14] use a time-varying connectedness approach to investigate the dynamics of return connectedness among crude oil, gold, and corn and stock, bond, and currency in China and the US. They find that, the total return of connectedness of the US commodity and financial assets are more robust than that of China and that both increased rapidly following the outbreak of the Covid-19 pandemic.

Yoon et al. [15] use the connectedness approach to investigate net return spillover between financial markets of stock, currency, and bond with oil and gold in the Asia Pacific Belt. Their research finds that the US stock market is the most critical contributor to the return spillover shock of the major stock markets in the Asia Pacific Belt, effectively reinforcing the importance of the US stock market. Adekoya and Oliyede [16] use TVP-VAR and causality-in-quantiles to investigate how the COVID-19 pandemic drives the spillover connectedness among US Dollar exchange rate, crude oil, gold, S&P 500, and Bitcoin. They find evidence of solid volatility across these markets

[1] Six major crude oil benchmarks are Brent, WTI, Dubai crude, Bonny Light, Tapis and OPEC basket reference.

and that gold, and the USD dollar are net receivers of shocks, while others are net transmitters. Many other empirical studies exist on the connectedness of commodities and financial markets. Among others, an interested researcher can also refer to [17–19]. For this brief chapter, we could not cover most empirical studies.

3. Data and methodology

3.1 Data

We use a daily dataset including credit default swaps (CDSs), exchange rates of South Africa (RD), gold prices, and platinum prices for the period of 05.01.2010–2017.06.2022. We transform the dataset into logarithmic return series before we start the empirical analysis stage. Hence, the descriptive statistic of our dataset is given in **Table 1**.

According to the kurtosis value in **Table 1**, which is the fourth moment, CDS has high variability, i.e., 54.68, compared to the kurtosis values of gold, platinum, and RD variables. This interpretation is valid for the entire data set since the other kurtosis values are all greater than three, i.e., 8.90; 9.42; 4.67, respectively.

Considering the skewness parameters in **Table 1**, which measure the asymmetry, the values of CDS and RD variables are greater than zero and are also positive. However, the asymmetry parameters of gold and platinum, i.e., the skewness values, reveal that the negative effects in these markets are more dominant than the positive effects. Notably, the skewness value of CDS, i.e., 2.28, appears as the financial risk indicator of South Africa, and the size of the asymmetric effect in the exchange rates seems to be an important indicator, as a country-specific condition. Therefore, the interconnectedness of these variables provides valuable information as an important financial risk indicator considering the South African economy. From this point of view, the results allow the analysis of the possible country risk according to the price movements in the international markets, while the feedback effects between the indicators of this can be seen. In this respect, the transition effect of the said negative effects from international markets to the country's financial risk indicator is calculated via CDS. The channel of transmission of this effect on the country's economy is through the exchange rates.

	CDS	GOLD	PLA	RD
Mean	1.000222	1.000152	0.999849	1.000244
Median	1.000000	1.000374	1.000032	0.999829
Maximum	1.598863	1.049666	1.100920	1.064441
Minimum	0.728329	0.904879	0.863620	0.949187
Std. Dev.	0.030376	0.009636	0.013902	0.009682
Skewness	2.287893	−0.637971	−0.562645	0.300564
Kurtosis	54.68895	8.905508	9.424978	4.670437
Jarque-Bera	364522.3	4941.601	5759.749	426.6634
Probability	0.000000	0.000000	0.000000	0.000000

Table 1.
Descriptive statistics of dataset for South Africa – (2010–2022).

Variables	ADF-C	ADF-NONC	KPSS-C	KPSS-Lin-Cos
CDS	−16.623*	−0.0742	0.0205*	0.0211*
GOLD	−56.838*	−0.0147	0.1102*	0.1059*
PLA	−24.606*	−0.0498	0.0438*	0.0391*
RD	−56.783*	−0.0409	0.0619*	0.0391*
%1—	−3.432	−2.565	0.739	0.216
%5–	−2.862	−1.940	0.463	0.146

**significant at 1% confidence level as I (0).*

Table 2.
Unit-root test results of South African daily return series (2010–2022).

Variables	Q(20)	$Q^2(20)$	ARCH Effects
CDS	21.52***	65.974**	54.37**
GOLD	9.51	252.34**	141.68**
PLA	12.74	995.84**	569.09**
RD	15.743	389.02**	225.58**

****Significant at 5% chi-square distribution.*
***Significant at 1% chi-square distribution.*

Table 3.
ARCH effects on return series.

It is seen that the kurtosis values of all the variables are greater than three, that there is a significant risk in these markets and that the possible risk may have a high impact on the country's economy through the financial risk indicator channel. The presence of asymmetric effects and kurtosis values higher than three indicate that there may be a time-varying parameter relationship between these variables. Based on this assumption, we proceed to the next step to apply TVP-VAR Model.

All the return series are stationary, based on the unit-root test results given in **Table 2**. Along with the Augmented Dickey-Fuller-ADF test [20], the Kwiatkowski-Phillips-Schmidt-Shin-KPSS test was also applied [21]. Thus, the test result, which may be due to the insensitivity to the possible degree of integration being less than one, was verified with the KPSS test. Therefore, the data are considered stationary as I (0), since the test results support the results of the ADF test with a constant.

The ARCH test and Ljung Box Test, applied up to 20 lags to determine the presence of fat tails in the return series. Hence, as shown in **Table 3**, the ARCH effect is statistically significant and shows the presence of time-varying volatility[2] and Ljung

[2] The ARCH test is a major instrument for determining the "conditional variance" based on the time dynamics of the second moments of the data. Hence, we could interpret a statistically significant ARCH test result as a representative of the time-varying volatility condition for the data. In addition, we could say that we have a volatility clustering with the existence of a fat-tailed distribution as a sign of mean reversion tendency in the return series. On the other hand, it should be noted that the existence of a significant excess kurtosis (i.e., excess kurtosis >0) is not representative of time-varying volatility. Still, the inverse of this hypothesis is true.

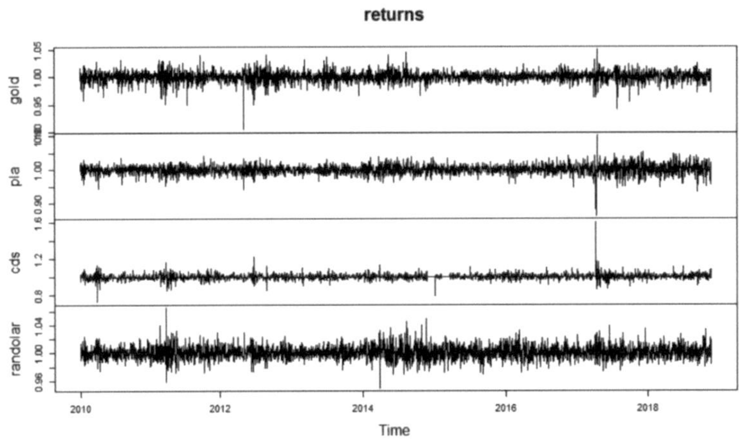

Figure 1.
Daily return series of gold, platinum, CDS, and RD (2010–2022).

Box test is used for analysing whether the specification is relevant to get "autocorrelation" and to capture the "time-varying volatility" in the return series.

After having the unit root test and ARCH test results, a daily percentage change of the dataset is prepared to determine absolute negative and positive return series. The dispersions of the daily change in return series are illustrated in **Figure 1**. In this respect, all the return series appear significantly skewed, and the JB test statistics support that these series are not normally distributed [22]. These initial descriptive findings of our return series support our method to apply TVP-VAR modelling with "time-varying variance-covariances".

3.2 Dynamic connectedness based time-varying vector autoregressive (TVPVAR) model

We use the "Time-Varying Parameter Vector-Autoregressive (TVP-VAR) Model" in our analysis because we aim to investigate the return-spillovers between the series. The brief literature review and the explanation of the TVP-VAR Model is given below.

This chapter applies the asymmetric dynamic interconnectedness approach to the South African financial time series data. This analysis is an extension of the empirical works of Diebold and Yılmaz [6–23]. These authors wrote the pioneering work regarding the development of "dynamic connectedness measures". In addition, we rely on the works of Antonakakis et al. [4] and, Kahyaoglu Bozkus and Kahyaoglu [24]. Antonakakis et al. [4] proposes a measure for dynamic connectedness, developed to evaluate time-varying parameter VAR models. In this way, they manage to cope with the drawbacks of the standard rolling-windows dynamic approach [25].

It is important to capture the asymmetries in the financial time analysis. In this respect, we calculate all the absolute returns both in positive and negative signs for our dataset. This calculation is essential for the TVP-VAR based connectedness approach [25]. In our case, we use TVP-VAR (1). This is suggested based on the Bayesian Information Criterion (BIC). Our approach is defined in Eqs. (1) and (2) as follows:

$$z_t = B_t z_{t-1} + u_t \qquad u_t \sim N\left(0, \sum\nolimits_t\right) \tag{1}$$

$$vec(B_t) = vec(B_{t-1}) + v_t \qquad v_t \sim N(0, R_t) \tag{2}$$

Where:

z_t and z_{t-1}	$k \times 1$ vector in t, $t - 1$ period.
u_t	the error term
B_t and $\sum_t$	$k \times k$ matrices with the time-varying VAR coefficients and the time-varying variance-covariances
$vec(B_t)$	$k^2 \times 1$ vector
v_t	$k^2 \times 1$ vector
R_t	$k^2 \times k^2$ matrix

According to the "Wold Representation Theorem" introduced by Pesaran and Shin [26], it is necessary to transform the estimated TVP-VAR model into its TVP-VMA process by using Eq. (3):

$$z_t = \sum_{i=1}^{p} B_{it} z_{t-i} + u_t = \sum_{j=0}^{\infty} A_{jt} u_{t-j} \tag{3}$$

The index for "pairwise directional connectedness", "total directional connectedness", "NET total directional connectedness" and "total connectedness index (TCI)" from j to i are formulated and obtained via R program based on the recent work of [27]. These authors define "influence variable (H) as forecast horizon" as follows:

$$\tilde{\varphi}^{g}_{ij,t}(H) = \frac{\tilde{\varphi}^{g}_{ij,t}(H)}{\sum_{j=1}^{k} \varnothing^{g}_{ij,t}(H)} \tag{4}$$

In this respect, we begin our analysis by determining the average connectedness measure, i.e., without considering asymmetry. It should be noted that all figures relate concurrently to both negative and positive returns and the symmetric connectedness measures. In other words, "off-diagonal factors" in the figures indicate the interaction between the variables in the system. On the other hand, the "elements in the main diagonal" match to "idiosyncratic shocks", namely, "own-innovations" for the series. The process is followed by applying Eq. (4) to calculate different cases based on the work of Kahyaoglu, Bozkus and Kahyaoglu [24] such that:

1. *Total directional connectedness TO others*: where variable i spreads its shock wave to all additional variables j, called total directional connectedness TO others.

2. *Total directional connectedness FROM others:* where the shock wave variable i gets from variables j.

3. *NET total directional connectedness*: where we calculate by deducting "the total directional connectedness TO others" from" the total directional connectedness FROM others." This indicates the "influence variable" i has on the examined system.

4. *Total connectedness index (TCI)*: This index is used as the final stage to see the whole market, i.e., the market interconnectedness.

5. *The pairwise connectedness index (PCI)*: TCI is decomposed to obtain the interconnectedness between two variables, i and j. According to Gabauer [27], PCI metrics range between [0, 1] and this shows the "degree of pairwise interconnectedness".

4. Empirical results analysis

We studied the effects of the daily changes in the prices of gold and platinum, two important export items from South Africa, on the country's financial risk indicator (CDS) and the exchange rates (RD). Our empirical findings from the asymmetric TVP-VAR Model connectedness analysis are as follows:

The empirical results of the TVP-VAR Model are obtained based on South Africa's return series for the examined period, and they are given in **Table 4**, and **Figure 2**, **Figure 3**, **Figure 4**, and **Figure 5**, respectively. In general, we monitor that the connectedness level in the network reaches high values between 2014 and 2016 and during early 2018 (**Figure 2**). Considering **Figure 2**, 2014, 2016 and 2018 seem to be prominent as the periods of shocks in South Africa. The country-specific events that occurred during these periods, triggering these effects, are summarised in **Table 5**.

After we make the prediction error variance decomposition, two critical pieces of information emerge. These are called variance shares, which originate from "internal shocks" and "external shocks". External shocks are also called "spillovers" in the literature. The connectedness results in **Table 4** constitute essential details, where all the relationships in the system can be defined to understand the "big picture", i.e., the South African case.

In this model, for each variable, Y-return, p-positive, and n-negative returns are shown at **Table 4**. The difference of negative and positive returns of the variables means the divergence of positive and negative effects in this model. Therefore, these effects are defined as "asymmetric" effects.

Notably, there is a spillover from the gold market to the platinum market. The value of (11.16) can be interpreted as a measure of this effect. In general, the positive and negative effects in the gold market do not have an asymmetrical effect on the gold market. This is underpinned by the findings that the gold's positive and negative returns are effectively at similar rates, i.e., gold. Yp (12.65) and gold. Yn (12.22) values are close to each other showing this fact. There is a similar situation occurring from the platinum market to the gold market. However, the gold market appears to be a higher shock receiver than the platinum market because the spread from pla.Y to gold. Y is (13.11), while the reverse spillover is at the level of (11.16).

The cds.Y variables receive the biggest shock from themselves. However, there is a difference between the positive and negative effects, considering the financial markets' perspectives of the South African economy. The positive and negative difference here is that the negative shock of cds.Y causes a faster increase than positive shocks, reflecting that the increase in CDSs will have a negative effect on the economy. Since cds.Yp expresses the positive shock increase direction in our CDS variable, it expresses the negative impact on the economy. From this point of view, the impact of the shock in international financial markets on South Africa is asymmetrical in both positive and negative directions. In this context, it is possible to say that the general effect of this

Variable	gold.Y	pla.Y	cds.Y	rd.Y	gold.Yp	pla.Yp	cds.Yp	rd.Yp	gold.Yn	pla.Yn	cds.Yn	rd.Yn	FROM
gold.Y	29.14	13.11	1.88	3.14	14.14	8.51	1.65	2.69	13.66	7.72	1.70	2.66	**70.86**
pla.Y	11.16	25.29	3.72	4.53	6.28	15.15	3.24	3.79	6.26	13.57	3.27	3.75	**74.71**
cds.Y	1.76	4.24	29.30	10.11	2.37	2.75	15.68	7.21	2.62	2.23	14.64	7.08	**70.70**
rd.Y	2.84	4.74	7.93	26.25	3.17	3.34	5.92	16.91	3.38	3.01	5.88	16.63	**73.75**
gold.Yp	12.65	6.60	2.27	3.34	26.33	5.88	2.19	3.31	26.22	5.66	2.24	3.30	**73.67**
pla.Yp	7.23	15.31	2.49	3.36	5.89	25.09	2.28	3.08	5.89	23.95	2.38	3.06	**74.91**
cds.Yp	1.54	3.61	14.56	6.69	2.45	2.63	26.72	6.23	2.73	2.08	24.61	6.13	**73.28**
rd.Yp	2.13	3.69	5.63	16.16	2.89	2.79	5.24	25.32	3.11	2.40	5.32	25.31	**74.68**
gold.Yn	12.22	6.52	2.41	3.44	26.12	5.81	2.37	3.41	26.32	5.58	2.41	3.39	**73.68**
pla.Yn	7.13	14.34	2.23	3.36	6.04	24.98	1.99	2.99	6.01	25.85	2.09	2.98	**74.15**
cds.Yn	1.60	3.65	13.71	6.62	2.54	2.74	24.71	6.27	2.82	2.18	27.00	6.18	**73.00**
rd.Yn	2.13	3.67	5.57	16.00	2.90	2.78	5.19	25.48	3.10	2.40	5.28	25.50	**74.50**
TO	**62.39**	**79.48**	**62.39**	**76.76**	**74.81**	**77.37**	**70.47**	**81.38**	**75.80**	**70.78**	**69.84**	**80.45**	**881.91**
Inc.Own	91.53	104.77	91.69	103.01	101.13	102.46	97.18	106.70	102.12	96.62	96.83	105.95	cTCI/TCI
NET	**−8.47**	**4.77**	**−8.31**	**3.01**	**1.13**	**2.46**	**−2.82**	**6.70**	**2.12**	**−3.38**	**−3.17**	**5.95**	80.17/73.49
NPT	**0.00**	**9.00**	**2.00**	**8.00**	**6.00**	**5.00**	**3.00**	**11.00**	**7.00**	**3.00**	**2.00**	**10.00**	

gold.Y-Return of Gold Series; pla.Y-Return of platinum series; cds.Y-Return of CDS; rd.Y-Return of RD series. gold.Yn-Negative Return of Gold Series; pla.Yn- Negative Return of platinum series; cds.Yn- Negative Return of CDS; rd.Yn- Negative Return of RD series gold.Yp-Positive Return of Gold Series; pla.Yp- Positive Return of platinum series; cds.Yp- Positive Return of CDS; rd.Yp-Positive Return of RD series, Inc.Own: Including own contributions, TCI:Total Connectedness Index, NET:Net Total Connectedness, NPT: Net Pairwise Total Connectedness.

Table 4.
Empirical findings of asymmetric connectedness analysis with TVP-VAR approach.

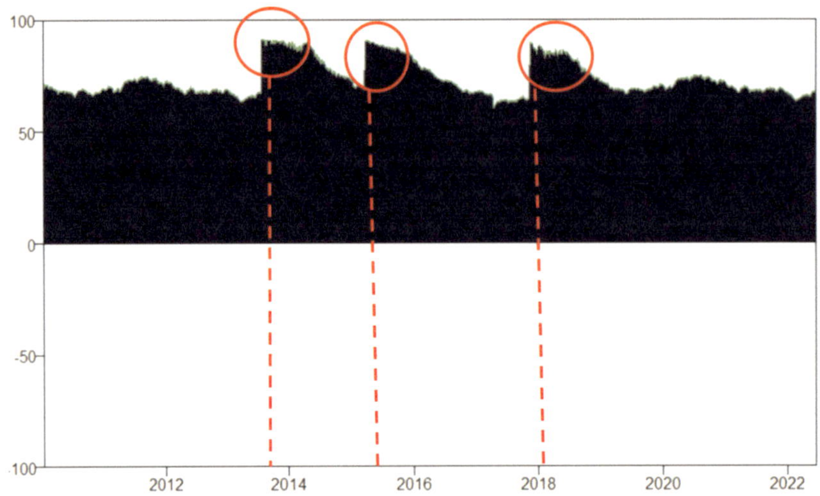

Figure 2.
Asymmetry of dynamic total connectedness. Note: Results are obtained from TVP-VAR model. This model is established with the lag length of order one (BIC). We use a 20-step-ahead "generalised forecast error variance decomposition".

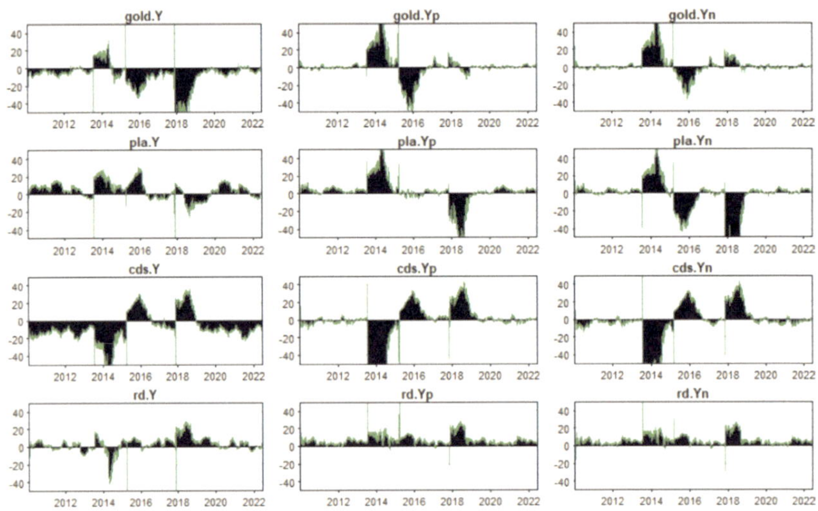

Figure 3.
Dynamic net total directional connectedness.

shock on the country's economy also shows an asymmetrical spillover on the exchange rates. However, this asymmetric effect does not differ much in terms of positive and negative effects on exchange rates. This is related to the fact that the shock of CDS (cds.Y) from exchange rate (rd.Y) is (10.11), which is greater than the shock of exchange rates (rd.Y) from CDS (cds.Y). For this reason, the effects of a shock, whether from exchange rates or CDSs, on CDSs after a period will be greater anyway.

The important point here is that there is a difference between the shock value of each variable from the total connectedness and the total shock of each positive and negative shock. Suppose this situation is considered as a difference in the spillover effects from the total connectedness to the positive and negative, and from the positive

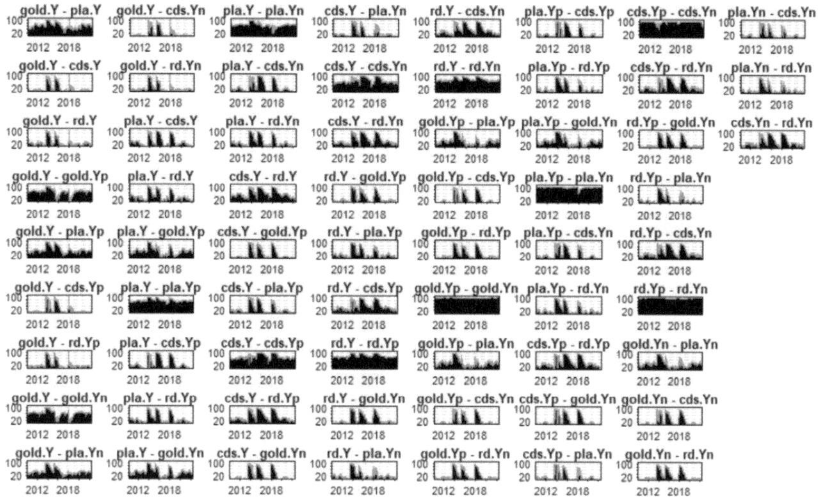

Figure 4.
Dynamic net pairwise directional connectedness. Notes: Results are obtained from TVP-VAR model. This model is established with the lag length of order one (BIC). We use a 20-step-ahead "generalised forecast error variance decomposition". Black area shows the symmetric pairwise connectedness. Green and red lines indicate the "positive and negative pairwise connectedness measures", respectively.

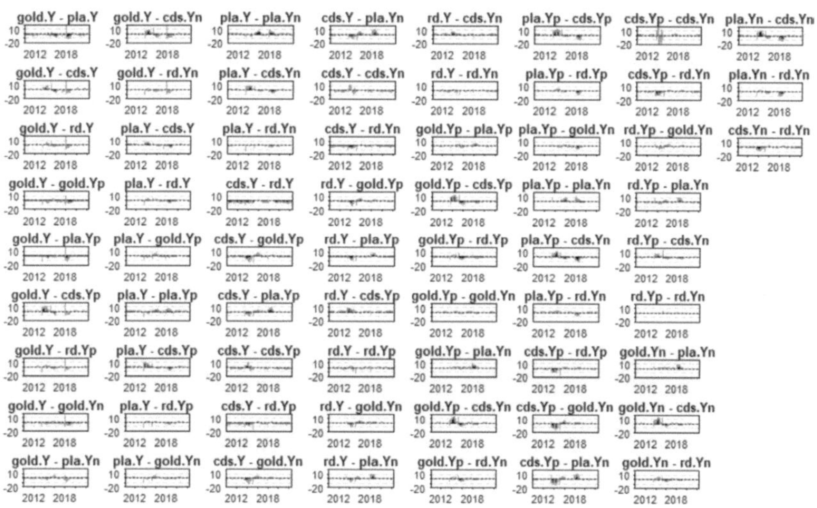

Figure 5.
Net pairwise directional connectedness.

and negative to the total connectedness. In that case, it is seen that there is a significant asymmetric effect due to the interaction between the exchange rates and CDS in South Africa. Considering the openness of the South African economy, novel monetary policy implementations are needed to manage this asymmetry. Within the framework of the knowledge that the CDSs are the main risk indicator in international markets, public finance should also be considered in the new regulation process in South Africa.

Even if the values in **Table 4** seem to be relatively close to each other when making interpretations, it should be considered that they are all obtained from daily data. The fact that the total connectivity among the data we have analysed is 73%, provides important information. The empirical findings of the study provide valuable

SA Specific Events	Negative	Positive
2018	Land reform constitution change announcement - Heightening policy uncertainty	Moody's affirmed SA credit rating
		Tito Mboweni appointed as Finance Minister
		Moody's upgrade SA outlook to stable
		Nhlanhla Nene appointed as Finance Minister
		Cyril Ramaphosa appointed as President
		Jacob Zuma resigns
2017	Heightened policy uncertainty around the Third Mining Charter release	Cyril Ramaphosa appointed as ANC president (54th Conference)
2016	Domestic drought, above-target inflation outcomes	
	SA lose investment grade (for foreign currency debt) with two of the three major rating agencies	
2015	"Nene-gate": Minister of Finance Nhlanhla Nene replaced by a relatively unknown Desmond van Rooyen	Four days later Pravin Gordon appointed as Finance Minister
	Electricity load shedding	
	Domestic drought, above-target inflation outcomes	
2014	African Bank experienced liquidity stress, generating risk across financial markets and risk of contagion	
	Widening current account deficit	

Source: Chatterjee and Sing [28], The World Bank [29], Authors.

Table 5.
Summary of negative and positive events in South Africa - 2014–2018.

information for the establishment of macro-financial stability policies and give reliable information about the future risk directions in the economy. This can be considered, especially regarding South Africa's presence in international financial markets with the country's main export items, which are the financialised commodities.

5. Conclusion

The gold, platinum, exchange rates, and CDS data of South Africa we have investigated can be seen as an early warning risk indicator for the economy. In this context, based on the TVP-VAR model, findings obtained for these indicators, expresses the asymmetric time-varying connectedness of the country's economy to international financial markets.

In general, gold and CDSs are the ones that give shocks to the system, while platinum and the exchange rates are the ones that take the shocks. When the positive

DOI: http://dx.doi.org/10.5772/intechopen.107248

and negative effects of each of the variables are examined, it is clearly seen that there is a difference in whether the system is shocked or not.

In the case of gold and the exchange rates, which are negative for the country, these variables are also shock receivers. This means that the positive and negative variables in question reveal a trend in the same direction for the country. However, the negative effects of CDSs and platinum, that is, an increase in CDSs, which is negative for the country, and changes in platinum prices are shock generating for the country.

An important point to note about CDSs is that shocks originating from the agricultural sector, which are not included in our model, but which are especially important for most countries, should also be taken into account. Assuming that the CDS data will be affected by such shocks, we can say that this connectivity may be effective in the country's economy due to its high value.

Net effects show asymmetric effects due to positive and negative interactions. The important finding here is that it should be emphasised that our model is valid with a time-varying approach. This necessitates institutional policies that will synchronise the reflections of these markets from an economic point of view. Considering that the important source of demand in the precious metals sector is affected by the Chinese economy, it can be stated that the growth trend of that economy should also be closely monitored.

Acknowledgements

We would like to thank the University of Johannesburg for funding the publication fees for our study.

We would like to also thank Prof. David Gabauer for his kind assistance by providing R codes.

Conflict of interest

"The authors declare no conflict of interest."

Author details

Lethiwe Nzama[1*], Thanda Sithole[2] and Sezer Bozkus Kahyaoglu[3,4,5]

1 University of Johannesburg, College of Business and Economics School of Accounting, Department of Commercial Accounting, Rossmore, Johannesburg, South Africa

2 Senior Economist, Johannesburg, South Africa

3 Izmir Bakircay University, Izmir, Turkiye

4 University of Johannesburg, Johannesburg, South Africa

5 Manas University, Bishkek, Kyrgyz Republic

*Address all correspondence to: lethiwen@uj.ac.za

References

[1] US Geological Survey. Mineral commodity summary. US Geological Survey; 2022. DOI: 10.3133/msc2022

[2] Bank for International Settlement. BIS Triennial central bank survey; 2019. Available from: https://www.bis.org/statistics/rpfx19_fx.htm

[3] Sayed A, Charteris A. Is the rand a commodity currency? A volatility spillover analysis. 2022. DOI: 10.1080/10293523.2022.2090079

[4] Antonakakis N, Chatziantoniou I, Gabauer D. Refined measures of dynamic connectedness based on time-varying parameter vector autoregressions. Journal of Risk and Financial Management. 2020;**13**(4):84. DOI: 10.3390/jrfm13040084

[5] Mensi W, Ali SR, Vinh VX, Kang S. Multiple dependence, spillovers, and connectedness between precious metals and currency markets: A safe haven analysis. SSRN. 2022. DOI: 10.2139/ssrn.4016986

[6] Diebold FX, Yılmaz K. On the network topology of variance decompositions: Measuring the connectedness of financial firms. Journal of Econometrics. 2014;**182**(1):119-134. DOI: 10.1016/j.jeconom.2014.04.012

[7] Antonakakis N, Kizys R. Dynamic spillovers between commodity and currency markets. International Review of Financial Analysis. 2015;**41**:303-319. DOI: 10.1016/j.irfa.2015.01.016

[8] Rikhotso PM, Simo-Kengne BD. Dependence structures between sovereign credit default swaps and global risk factors in BRICS countries. Risk and Financial Management. 2022:15-109. DOI: 10.3390/jrfm15030109

[9] de Boyrie ME, Pavlova I. Dynamic interdependence of sovereign credit default swaps in BRICS and MIST countries. Applied Economics. 2016;**48**: 563-575. DOI: 10.1080/00036846.2015.1083089

[10] Simonyan S, Bayraktar S. Asymmetric dynamics in sovereign credit defaults swaps pricing: Evidence from emerging countries. International Journal of Emerging Markets. 2022. Available from. DOI: https://www.emerald.com/insight/1746-8809.htm

[11] Miranda-Agrippino Silvia, Hélène Rey, Chapter 1 - The global financial cycle. Gita Gopinath, Elhanan Helpman, Kenneth Rogoff. editors. In: Handbook of International Economics, Vol. 6. Elsevier; 2022. pp. 1-43. ISSN: 1573-4404, ISBN: 9780323957724. DOI: 10.1016/bs.hesint.2022.02.008

[12] Stéphane Z. New evidence on international risk-sharing in the economic community of West African States (ECOWAS). International Economics. 2021;165:121-139. ISSN: 2110-7017. DOI: 10.1016/j.inteco.2020.11.003

[13] Chatziantoniou I, Gabauer D, Gupta R. Integration and risk transmission in the market for crude oil: A time-varying parameter frequency connectedness approach. Working Paper, June 2021-47. University of Pretoria, Department of Economics, Pretoria, Gauteng, South Africa. Available from: https://www.up.ac.za/media/shared/61/WP/wp_2021_47.zp209709.pdf

[14] Li X, Li B, Wei G, Bai L, Wei Y, Liang C. Return connectedness among commodity and financial assets during

the COVID-19 pandemic: Evidence from China and the US. Resources Policy. 2021;**73**. DOI: 10.1016/j.resourpol.2021.102166

[15] Yoon SM, Mamun M, Uddin GS, Kang SH. Network connectedness and net spillover between financial and commodity markets. The North American Journal of Economics and Finance. 2019;**48**:801-818. DOI: 10.1016/j.najef.2018.08.012

[16] Adekoya OB, Oliyede JA. How COVID-19 drives connectedness among commodity and financial markets: Evidence from TVP-VAR and causality-in-quantiles technique. Resources Policy. 2021;**70**. DOI: 10.1016/j.resourpol.2020.101898

[17] Mensi W, Vo XV, Kang SH. Time and frequency connectedness and network across the precious metal and stock markets: Evidence from top precious metal importers and exporters. Resources Policy. 2021;**72**. DOI: 10.1016/j.resourpol.2021.102054

[18] Bouri E, Cepni O, Gabauer D, Gupta R. Return connectedness across asset classes around the COVID-19 outbreak. International Review of Financial Analysis. 2021;**73**. DOI: 10.1016/j.irfa.2020.101646

[19] Zhang D, Broadstock DC. Global financial crisis and rising connectedness in the international commodity markets. International Review of Financial Analysis. 2020;**68**. DOI: 10.1016/j.irfa.2018.08.003

[20] Dickey D, Fuller W. Distribution of the estimators for autoregressive time series with a unit root. Journal of the American Statistical Association. 1979;**74**:427-431. DOI: 10.1080/01621459.1979.10482531

[21] Kwiatkowski D, Phillips PCB, Schmidt P, Shin Y. Testing the null hypothesis of stationarity against the alternative of a unit root. Journal of Econometrics. 1992;**54**:159-178. DOI: 10.1016/0304-4076(92)90104-Y

[22] Jarque CM, Bera AK. Efficient tests for normality, homoscedasticity and serial independence of regression residuals. Economics Letters. 1980;**6**(3): 255-259. DOI: 10.1016/0165-1765(80)90024-5

[23] Diebold FX, Yılmaz K. Better to give than to receive: Predictive directional measurement of volatility spillovers. International Journal of Forecasting. 2012;**28**:57-66. DOI: 10.1016/j.ijforecast.2011.02.006

[24] Kahyaoglu Bozkus S, Kahyaoglu H. Financial connectedness of energy and commodity markets and systemic risk. In: Hacioglu U, Aksoy T, editors. Financial Ecosystem and Strategy in the Digital Era. Contributions to Finance and Accounting. Springer, 2021. Champions. DOI: 10.1007/978-3-030-72624-9_5

[25] Adekoya OB, Akinseye A, Antonakakis N, Chatziantoniou I, Gabauer D, Oliyide JA. Crude oil and Islamic sectoral stocks: Asymmetric connectedness and investment strategies. 2021. DOI: 10.1016/j.resourpol.2022.102877

[26] Pesaran MH and Shin Y. An autoregressive distributed-lag modelling approach to cointegration analysis. In: Econometrics and Economic Theory in the 20th Century: The Ragnar Frisch Centennial Symposium. Vol. 31. 1998. pp. 371-413. DOI: 10.1017/CCOL0521633230.011

[27] Gabauer D. Dynamic measures of asymmetric & pairwise spillovers within an optimal currency area: Evidence from

the ERM I System. Journal of Multinational Financial Management. 2021:100680. DOI: 10.1016/j.mulfin.2021.100680

[28] Chatterjee S, Sing M. Measuring Systemic Risk in South African Banks. Working Papers 11004, South African Reserve Bank. 2021

[29] The World Bank. South Africa Economic Update; Jobs and Inequality. The World Bank. 2018. Available from: https://thedocs.worldbank.org/en/doc/798731523331698204-0010022018/original/SouthAfricaEconomicUpdateApril2018.pdf